BALTIMORE GLIMPSES
Revisited

By
GILBERT SANDLER

Illustrated and
Edited by
IRV YANIGER

© 1984 by I.C.Y. Publishing Co.
4904 Old Court Road
Randallstown, MD 21133

ISBN 0-9613721-0-9

TABLE OF CONTENTS

BALTIMORE GLIMPSES REVISITED
by Sandler and Yaniger

IRV YANIGER
1933–1984

IRV YANIGER, who drew the Glimpses' cartoons from May of 1982 through Tuesday, September 25, 1984, died Friday, September 28, 1984, and it is altogether fitting that this book be dedicated to his memory. His first cartoon illustrated the Glimpses' story of Baltimore's famous escape artist, Jack Hart; his last, the "Storm of the Century" that devastated Ocean City 22 years ago. However, he brought much more to Glimpses than mere cartoons. His passion was to "get it right," as he used to put it, wryly challenging some fact or idea I had written in a particular Glimpse. "The whole idea, Sandler," he would say, "is to get it right." He believed that in every stone there is a statue; he would take a Baltimore Glimpses' manuscript and brood about it for hours, sometimes days. It was not in him just to draw one more cartoon to sort of "go with" the writing. He had to make his cartoon stand up and sing in harmony with the writing—not only supporting it and explaining it but lighting it up with that peculiar genius he had for getting it right. I occasionally suggested to him that his work was too cerebral for many of our readers, and that often they may not have appreciated the nuances of his efforts. "That problem," he would respond, "is the reader's. Mine is to get it right." Though he worked well and successfully in many art forms—layout, design, typography, illustration—his first love was cartooning. It was his dream to see his own cartoon strip carried some day in a major newspaper. I have no doubt that had he lived he would have seen that dream come true. He was that good. All this that I have written about Irv is based on what I have come to realize over my long years of friendship with him. I just hope I got it right.

Gilbert Sandler
October, 1984

PREFACE
by Gwinn Owens
Editor, Other Voices, The Evening Sun

EARLY IN 1979 *The Evening Sun* was making plans to launch its first op-ed page. Bradford Jacobs, then editorial page editor, hired me to take charge of the new venture. In the weeks before the page was launched we chose a name ("Other Voices") and culled through the available features and columnists, deciding what to use and what to discard. In only one case was there absolutely no doubt: *Baltimore Glimpses*, which had made its debut four years earlier on the editorial page, would be continued on the new page with a larger and more decorative format.

No wonder; this capsulized nostalgia uniquely preserved the Baltimore that existed before the age of electronic communication and high speed travel began to shake American cities down to a common denominator. Here was a city so isolated, unvisited and ingrown that its folklore was both provincial and precious. Even in today's more cosmopolitan Baltimore, with its daily busloads of tourists, this appealing provinciality is not completely gone. Gil Sandler preserves not only what we were, but to some extent what we should strive to keep.

For many years there was what seemed to be an almost indispensible partnership between Sandler and John Stees, the gifted *Evening Sun* cartoonist who captured Gil's message in a few simple lines. Then, sadly and suddenly, more than two years ago, John Stees died. As an editor I was personally grieved and professionally troubled. Who could replace Stees? I envisioned months of searching.

It was Gil Sandler himself who suggested an uncelebrated artist-cartoonist named Irv Yaniger. In desperation—the need was immediate—I called this Irv Yaniger to see if he would do a cartoon or two to fill in the gap. Irv's first cartoon was a gem; so was every one that followed. There was no gap. Now, Yaniger pictures are almost as much a fixture of *Baltimore Glimpses* as Sandler words.

And, happily, Irv's enthusiasm has carried *Baltimore Glimpses* into the extra dimension of this book. Henceforth, these priceless time-warp snippets are available from the bookshelf, more or less forever. That's how it should be.

INTRODUCTION

FOR MORE THAN A DECADE now, Gil Sandler has been recalling that portion of Baltimore's history too recent for the textbooks and too long ago for the news. The newspaper column called *Baltimore Glimpses*, scribbled by that same Gilbert Sandler, has appeared in the *Evening Sun* every Tuesday during all that time.

The column has proved to be among the most popular, and among the longest running, of any in the Sunpapers. Indeed, it has been appearing for so long that many events which were hot news in the early days of *Baltimore Glimpses* now qualify for the column themselves.

It is so popular that it has a fan club. Loosely organized, of course. It meets on occasional Tuesdays to discuss this week's column, detect errors of fact in it, and to upbraid the author for his carelessness. They never ask for a retraction or a reprint, so their motive is evidently the pure pleasure of humiliating the man.

Not content with badgering him about his errors, people from all over Baltimore keep sending him things—old streetcar transfers, programs from the International League Orioles, milk bottles from long-dead dairies that once delivered door to door. His cup overfloweth.

Dr. Morgan Pritchett, Director of the Maryland Room of the Pratt Library, calls the columns "valuable history" and keeps a collection on hand for scholars.

You, dear reader, need not be a scholar to enjoy the full bouquet of the Sandler prose style. Just dive into this selection of Baltimore's Best. You'll find 66 editions of *Glimpses* in the first part of the book.

The last part of the book is a collection of Baltimore Trivia Quizzes, culled from Gil's annual contests. You'll have fun with those, even if you get most of the answers wrong.

Here they are, Baltimore. Enjoy them again.

CITIES ALL ALIKE (EXCEPT ONE)

EDITOR'S NOTE: The following piece is probably the right one to begin this collection with, since it has so much to say about Baltimore's unique qualities. Ironically, it caused a furor when it appeared, because of the word "downayshin." Gil always thought this was the real Balamorene way to refer to a trip to the beach. He was promptly disabused of that belief. Proper Balamorenes reminded him that they always went "downashore" in the summer. He apologized and corrected himself in a later column, but the purity of his original version is preserved here.

REGIONAL DIFFERENCES are disappearing; cities are beginning to look alike, even sound alike. You've had the telling experience. Ride out of any airport into any town and what do you see? The highway signs look alike—white lettering on green. The golden arches are there, and the Holiday Inn signs. In your hotel, turn the TV on and catch the local news. There is the same good-looking anchor man or woman, and the same nice-guy sportscaster with the open collar. The same weatherman is toying with his electronic high-pressure areas.

Blame this sameness on what we call progress. It is cheaper to make all signs and all buildings alike than it is to create them differently. And modern-day mass migration is responsible for the sameness of language and lifestyle. So many people are born in one city and come to live in another that their local culture is lost in the merge.

Ah, but some cities are holding out against the onslaught, standing fast and firm against the winds of change. Baltimore is one of them.

We flaunt our white steps, our steamed crabs and our funny way of talking. We still seem to call power mowers "paramours" and pavements "payments" and still, every Friday afternoon in the summer, go "downayshin." About those white steps: the best explanation of how we got them is that builders began to use the marble being hauled from Baltimore County quarries during the years when the city was building the

Washington Monument. But a lot of those white marble steps are really wood. Matter of fact, over in Fells Point some of those wooden steps used to be portable. Residents, when retiring for the night, either turned them over or took them inside.

We can trace Baltimore's reputation as "Crabtown" (a name once applied more often to Annapolis) back to 1915, and to two Eastern Shoremen, Zack Windsor and John Leonard. They had been shipping canned crab meat to Baltimore, but knew that Shoremen had been steaming live crabs and eating the meat right out of the shell. They thought of trying to sell this shore style of crab-eating to Baltimore townsfolk. Obviously, the idea worked.

Baltimorese is supposed to be made up of an outrageous mixture of Southern Cracker, Pennsylvania Dutch sing-song, and Cockney. We have former *Evening Sun* columnist John Goodspeed to thank for this Balmer accent story:

Seems that during the Battle of The Bulge in WWII, military police suspected an Army Lieutenant from Baltimore of being a German spy in American uniform—of which there were reported to be many in the sector then. But an MP from The Big Crab heard the lieutenant pronounce the name of his town—and passed him as genuine.

People can travel this country over and back again, and in the process make one city look and sound like another. But if anybody wants the special feeling that comes with sitting out on white marble steps—or being downayshin—and eatin' steamers, they will have to come to Balmer.

WHEN IT WAS "OUR" CITY

H ENRY "GRANDPA" SNOW is 93, and Baltimore born and bred. He is retired now, of course, and spends most of his time sitting on the porch of his Roland Park home telling stories to friends. But in earlier years he was active in business and in the life of the city.

He is old enough to remember the Baltimore Fire of 1904, and how the town rebuilt itself, and lived and worked and played between the Great Wars, and after them, too. He speaks wistfully of the differences the years have made in the life of the city—at least for him.

"Back then, you see, there was a feeling among Baltimoreans that they owned Baltimore—what there was of it, anyway." What there was of it, Mr. Snow goes on to explain, were the amenities of city life as Baltimoreans knew them in the 30's and 40's and 50's.

He means baseball at Oriole Park before a capacity crowd of 12,000. He means excursions down the bay to Tolchester. He means streetcar rides to amusement parks—Bay Shore and Carlin's and Gwynn Oak.

"We felt those things were ours. But it's different today," he says. "The National Aquarium, Harborplace, the Science Center, the zoo—that's all big business now. Tourists come to visit them by the millions." (We refrained from informing Mr. Snow that on a certain Sunday more people visited Harborplace than Disneyland.)

"So all those places no longer belong to Baltimoreans. They belong to the tourists and, I guess, to the world. We had concerts in the park, rowing on the Druid Hill Park boat lake, City-Poly football, Thanksgiving Day Toytown Parades. They were ours.

"Why, you could be standing on the curb watching the Toytown Parade and strike up a conversation with the guy next to you and you'd ask where he's from, and he'd tell you and you'd say, putting him on, 'DUN-dalk?'

"Now you stand in line at the Aquarium and you find the guy next to you is from Chicago, or Paris, or Jakarta. Nobody blinks. It's all a good thing, of course, the city needs it. Industry. Jobs. All good. But still, I miss the Baltimore that used to be ours."

So let's have two rousing cheers for the Baltimore of the Renaissance—and one small one, too, please (maybe just the echo of one) for the Baltimore of Grandpa Snow. His Baltimore is worth remembering, as well. After all, if you want to know where you are, it's nice to know where you've been.

"BANK DAY"
IN THE SCHOOLS

PICTURE YOURSELF in elementary school No. 59, or 18, or 64 in the 1930's or '40's or '50's—depending on where and when you went to elementary school in Baltimore City. It is Friday morning, and something unusual is going on in the classrooms. Students are all standing in a line among rows of seats leading to a single desk where two or three students are busy accepting pennies and nickels and dimes and quarters, and receipting them in bank books.

It is Bank Day, and the kids are lined up as they are every Friday morning at this time to deposit their week's savings into one of Baltimore's mutual savings banks through the Baltimore City School Bank Program. The program was started in 1924 "to teach thrift to our young people," a cooperative effort of the Baltimore City School Board and Association of Mutual Savings Banks of Baltimore. Every Friday morning more than half of the kids in each class would be banking their coins.

"The success of the program," Dr. David Weglein, School Superintendent during the 1930's said, "has long exceeded our expectations." In 1924 the total deposited was $7,072; in 1925 it had mushroomed to $86,195; in 1931 to $96,221. And believe it or not, in the early 1930's in the heart of the Great Depression, the kids continued to keep up their deposits, sending the total to over $150,000.

In 1960, when economics dictated that the system be discontinued, the total exceeded $3,000,000, with more than 50 elementary schools in the program.

It wasn't only the savings habit that endeared the program to the schools, parents and the city, it was the training. "Children perform all of the banking duties," Dr. Weglein explained. "They take the money, fill out the bank books with deposits and withdrawals, and keep the lines straight and moving. Perfect discipline prevails."

If you went to elementary school in Baltimore City anytime from the 1930's through the 1950's, you surely remember Bank Day, and saving your money week by week, year after year. If you can remember that, can you remember one more thing? Can you remember what happened to all that money you saved?

SCHOOL 49

NATIONAL COMMISSION on Excellence in Education
Washington, D.C.

Dear Mesdames and Messrs:

We see by the news that you have issued a devastating report on how bad things are with schools in America today. The report says that the teachers aren't teaching and the kids aren't learning and the parents aren't parenting, and there may be too much sports and not enough homework.

Well, had you visited Baltimore in 1956 or so and sat in a classroom at P.S. 49, you wouldn't be going around saying things like that. "49" was Baltimore City's accelerated junior high school. The students did three years in two, and they were the best and the brightest from Baltimore's elementary schools.

School 49 (alias Robert E. Lee School) was founded in 1909 at 1205 Cathedral Street where it closed its doors in 1960. It was a no-nonsense all academic prep school open to everyone, but its students—only 400 of them at any one time—had to have an IQ of at least 110 and exceptional grades.

The school offered few extracurricular activities—no auditorium, no shops, no dramatics, no sports (although there was a small gym). But if there were few extracurricular activities, there was plenty of homework—at least three hours of it every night. A reporter visiting the school in the fall of 1957 was to write that the students started their day with the usual Pledge of Allegiance, only they did it in Latin:

Fidem meam obligo vexillo Civitatum Americae Foederatarum et rei publicae pro qua stat. Unae natione non dividendae, cum libertate justitiaque omnibus.

And now, NCEE Commissioners, for the point of this letter. If this were 1957 and you were to go around saying these nasty things about our schools, you would have heard from four hundred 12-and-13-year-old kids at School 49 in Baltimore. They would have let you have it but good—and in Latin, too.

ARE WE NORTHERN
OR SOUTHERN?

READERS ARE FOREVER asking us that old chestnut of a question: "Is Baltimore a Southern or a Northern city?" By way of defining terms, identify Northern with "fast-paced" and Southern with "slow-paced" and, well, let's see now.

The Orleans Street viaduct was opened to traffic on January 3, 1936, but yellowed records of the Old Town Merchants Association, the long-time chief boosters for the project, show the plans for the viaduct to have been in the making as early as 1895. So, 40 years to build the Orleans Street viaduct.

The Civic Center was abuilding, in successive but unsuccessful attempts, since 1912. It was to have been in Mt. Royal, then Federal Hill, then Pimlico Race Track, then Lake Clifton, then Druid Hill Park (see page 50 for the full story). It finally opened in 1962 at Baltimore Street and Hopkins Place—50 long years after it was conceived.

The idea of, and plan for, a subway system for Baltimore was presented to the city fathers in 1920. It was to begin its route (heading south) in Mt. Washington and roll under Roland Avenue and University Parkway to St. Paul and Franklin Streets—its "Grand Central Exchange" where other subway lines would fan out in all directions. But from the time the dreamers dreamed their underground dream until the day in late summer of 1983 when you could take your first subway ride in Baltimore, 53 years went by.

At about noon on June 30, 1952, cars started streaking across the new Chesapeake Bay Bridge, hailed that fine day as the third largest over-the-water span in the world. But the planning for it began in 1907, when a Baltimore merchant named Peter Campell suggested that a bridge to carry streetcar traffic from what used to be Bay Shore Park (but is now Bethlehem Yards at Sparrows Point) be built across the bay to Tolchester Beach. Before that bridge was opened in 1952, and because of it, some men would grow rich, others would become powerful; others would be left powerless and broke, and the lives of millions would be affected.

The records now shows that it took 45 controversial years to build the Civic Center, 53 years to build the subway, 45 to build the Bay Bridge. So let's hear that question again: "Is Baltimore a Northern ("fast-paced") or a Southern ("slow-paced") city?"

What y'all think naow?

PASSING OF
THE SNOWBALL

AWAY OF LIFE in Baltimore is passing. The famous Baltimore "snowball"—that delicious confection of shaved ice in a paper cup, flavored with chocolate or cherry, or grape, or whatever, and often topped with marshmallow—the one and only snowball is doomed to become one with the Tolchester Boat, the streetcar, and horseback riding in Druid Hill Park.

As is the custom in this city that remembers its lost heroes and institutions by erecting monuments, there needs to be a monument of a special kind and in a special place erected to the snowball. More about that later.

"Is it possible," you ask, "that there will be no snowball stands to be seen curbside in the neighborhoods? No snowballs for sale at the corner drugstore? No relief, heavenly and cooling, on those hot, wet August Baltimore nights?"

All very likely. The reason (hence the monument, and where it must be): Dave Davidson died. Mr Davidson was the inventor of the *Snowmaster* snowball-making machine that you saw wherever you bought a snowball. His wonderful machine did away with the hand-held ice shaver and made it possible to make snowballs faster and with a more consistent texture. In so doing, the *Snowmaster* made Baltimore the snowball capital of America. (The snowball idea quickly spread to other cities, where they were called "Snow Cones" or "Slush Cones.")

When Mr. Davidson died, the family closed the business. Its building, the famous "Snowmaster Building" at 124 Hopkins Place (on the west side between Lombard and Pratt) was standing in the way of the city's Inner Harbor Development. The Davidson family still owns the patents to the *Snowmaster,* and are willing to sell them.

But no more *Snowmasters* are being made, and when the ones now in use break down, they cannot be repaired or replaced, and so—believe it or not—it is only a matter of time before snowballs melt into history in Baltimore and anywhere else in America.

Now, if that seems not to be a very large matter to you, you must not be a

Baltimorean who remembers the taste of a chocolate snowball topped with marshmallow, lovingly put together for you on a summer evening by an enterprising 14-year-old.

But if, with us, you sense the epoch sighing its sad farewell, then you will join in the movement to have the city erect a very special kind of monument—a 3-story high replica of a snowball, shaved ice brimming over it, chocolate flavored and topped with a dollop of marshmallow—right on the site of the Snowmaster Building at 124 Hopkins Place.

There it will take its place in the city's psyche, along with the fountains in McKeldin Park, the sculpture in Federal Courthouse Plaza, and the plaque on the old Southern Hotel. If you won't have your snowball, at least you are entitled to the memory of it.

TUNNEL JOE

MARYLAND PENITENTIARY officials, according to a recent news report, caught an inmate who was trying to escape by building a tunnel out of the place. He had already dug 20 feet downward and outward, toward the prison yard and freedom. The inmate, unidentified, was not the first prisoner to attempt to tunnel out of the jail on the Fallsway. He is at least the third.

The first, and most spectacular, was "Tunnel Joe" Holmes, who actually made it. On the cold night of February 18, 1951, Joe pushed through the dirt that made up the narrow strip of lawn between the penitentiary and Eager Street, and felt the cool, free air. In moments he was on his way, walking down Eager Street.

His underground odyssey began the night of July 8, 1949, when, serving the eighth year of a 20-year sentence, he began scratching away at the concrete floor of his cell with a piece of metal. He planned to dig (to a depth, it turned out, of 26 feet) to a point where he could tunnel horizontally under the jail itself and beyond the wall, where he would surface precisely in the narrow lawn strip between the pen and Eager Street.

Holmes thought of everything. He acquired tools and a lamp, learned how to dispose of dirt down the commode, and thought to conceal noise by digging while the prison radio played. He accumulated money and clothes for use after his escape. The plan worked with uncanny perfection.

"Genius!" said Joe's admirers. "He thought of everything!" Well, not quite. On March 3, Joe was arrested in a holdup near the Washington Monument, and in minutes he was back in his cell. What happened?

"I went to Philadelphia," Joe said, "to get a job, but I couldn't. So I came back to get a ship out. If I had gotten a job I never would have come back and got caught."

And why couldn't Joe get a job? He had forgotten to get a Social Security card.

If Joe were alive today he would no doubt be cheering this modern-day tunneler,

and have some fatherly instructions for him. First he would tell him how to build a tunnel that would really get a man out, and second, he would give him this reminder: "Your Social Security Card! Don't leave jail without it!"

EDITOR'S NOTE: "Tunnel Joe" was only a one-timer. He was patient, he was persistent, he was energetic; but evidently, he put everything he had into that one tunnel. My own affections go to an earlier prison artist, Jack Hart, who . . . well, let Gil tell it. He does it so much better than I.

JACK HART'S
ESCAPES

L ATE IN THE AFTERNOON of March 14, 1955, a crowd of reporters, camera-men, uniformed guards, and the simply curious were milling about the door-way of the Maryland penitentiary on Preston Street. Something very big was happening. James Connelly, alias James "Red" Kelly, alias Jack Hart was about to step blinking into the sunlight, out of prison and into a life of freedom—ending an on-again, off-again prison career that had started 31 years before when Hart was a teenager, and giving us a story that ought to put into perspective today's news about the "spectacular" escapes from Maryland's penal institutions. These small-time escapees, breaking out humdrum as they do, couldn't carry Hart's bag of files and saw blades.

Hart not only escaped from the pen, he escaped twice, and on the morning of January 24, 1923, when he was first confined to the Maryland penitentiary for complicity in the famous Norris murder, he told Warden Patrick Brady flat out that he knew "six sure ways to escape." He was to try four of them, and two were to prove successful.

In May of 1923 he set the prison upside down by hiding for fourteen days in a hole he had dug in the prison wall. When he was discovered he was wearing civilian clothes and had money in his pocket.

On January 4, 1924 he escaped, beating a prison bedcount by using a dummy in his bed. His method of departure, through the prison and out, remains to this day unclear. He was free until December 24, 1924 when he was arrested in Chicago for his role in a robbery and returned to the Maryland penitentiary, over the objections of the Chicago police, who were suspicious of the security arrangements here. "No Mary-land prison," they claimed, "could hold Jack Hart."

For the next three years Hart was a "sore problem" to penitentiary officials. Guards were always finding saws and files in his cell, along with partially completed duplicate keys. In 1926 he cut a hole in his cell's slate floor and almost made it out again.

But on March 15, 1929, make it out again he did. He sawed through three locks in his cell door, cut through the ventilator with a can opener and made it over the wall to Preston Street using a rope made of bed sheets.

He was arrested in 1932 in Chicago (again) for shooting a man in a card game and was returned once again to the Maryland penitentiary. From there on out he became a model prisoner, earning his parole 33 years after he was originally sentenced—and then he left it all behind him.

Hart went first to work in the hospital in Sabillasville in Frederick County, and then went to live with his brother in New Jersey, where Hart died some years later.

All of today's wardens and guards and legislators worried sick by all of these recent prisoner escapes—all of them who think they have it rough now, they don't know how easy their lives really are. Jack Hart is dead.

NATES AND LEON'S COUNTER

THE PIMLICO HOTEL IS MOVING . . .
—News Item, *The Evening Sun*

On the afternoon of August 15, 1967, auctioneer Leon Zalis was standing in the middle of the now empty and cavernous restaurant on North Avenue near Linden, once known as Nates and Leon's. His impassioned pleas for bids brought no response. Herman Levy, who had come to buy, said, "I ain't got the heart to bid on anything."

The specific merchandise on the block at this very moment in the history of Baltimore was the famous glass counter which, in its glory days, displayed trays filled to overflowing with chopped liver and chicken salad.

"Wipe your tears, friends," Zalis begged. "Make a bid."

Finally and at long last, a bid for the case came — at $5. It took the counter, and all its memories. That is how Nates and Leon's, which had opened in 1937, closed in 1967.

Earlier, in 1950, partner Leon Shavitz had left to open shop in the smallish, sort of run-down Pimlico Hotel on Park Heights Avenue in Pimlico where, in his own way, he was carrying on the same style, dressed up a little for the uptown crowd.

Nates and Leon's, for most of the years from its 1937 opening until it closed with the ignominious sale of its famous counter for a measly $5, was one of the few restaurants in Baltimore serving 24 hours a day, seven days a week. The hours it was open was only one of the reasons why Nates and Leon's was a prime favorite with the old and the young, the bookies and the debutantes of the '30's through the '50's.

"The other reason," Nates Herr used to say, "was the food. You take that Number 3 sandwich. Corned beef, Russian dressing and cole slaw on rye bread. 25 cents. Everything fresh. No substitutes. No premixes. Never been beat." The prices weren't bad, either. A 1950 menu shows a corned beef sandwich for 30 cents; a whole prime rib steak dinner, $4.25.

Nates and Leon's traced its origins to the day when Nates, fresh out of World War I and Fort Holabird, started a ticket agency of sorts, working out of the Baltimore Street restaurants. He got to like the restaurant business and soon had a job with Becker's Restaurant at 921 West North Avenue. When the property down the street at 850 became available, he and an old friend from Brookfield Avenue, Leon Shavitz, bought it and started Nates and Leon's.

Now the Pimlico Hotel, carrying with it all its memories from the '30's and later, has moved to grander spaces on Reisterstown Road at Hooks Lane. How grand? Nates and Leon's on North Avenue held 45 seated customers; when Leon opened the Pimlico Hotel it seated 150 in the restaurant and bar; when the Park Heights Avenue establishment was closed, it could seat 350; the new facility seats 450.

In the new Pimlico Hotel the same $5 that once bought the entire display case that held all the sandwich meat that was ready for all the customers in the entire Nates and Leon's at any given time—that same $5 will get you a dish of, say, clams casino, or an egg roll.

Nates Herr and Leon Shavitz, just a couple of guys off of Brookfield Avenue who decided to open a restaurant on North Avenue in 1937, should be alive to see it.

EDITOR'S NOTE: There's more to be said about Nates and Leon's, and I'll give you some more Gil Sandler on that topic just below. But I can't let the opportunity pass without pointing out how casually he made the reference to a quintessentially Baltimorean address in the charming piece you have just read—921 West North Avenue. Where but in Baltimore, where High Street meets Low Street and where you can live on East West Street.

But enough digression. Read on for further information about Nates and Leon's, among others.

LIFE IN THE
WEE HOURS

HERE'S *BALTIMORE GLIMPSES'* Very Own Guide to Baltimore-After-Dark, circa 1960, with apologies to the *Sun Magazine's* Guide of the same name of September 18, 1983.

First, a lament. The problem with the restaurants recommended by the *Sun's* Guide is that, good as those restaurants are, the sissies all close down at 2 A.M. In the 1960's and earlier, 2 A.M. was about when, for the Baltimore cognoscenti of those days, Baltimore-After-Dark really began.

After the night clubs (the Copa, the Chanticleer, the Club Charles, the Blue Mirror) closed, you headed for, say, Nates and Leon's up on North Avenue. At 3 in the morning you were lucky to find a table. Nates used to say, "That wasn't just because we were open. It was the food. Our Number 3 sandwich—corned beef, cole slaw, Russian dressing on warm rye bread—25 cents. Never been beat."

He was partly right, but there was also the ambience. The place was uptown headquarters for people who live in the night—bookies, show people, businessmen cutting deals, teen-agers after school dances.

If you couldn't get a table there, you could head downtown to Howard and Fayette and spend your quarter at Thompson's. Ronald Flitt, who for many years had an all-night news-stand at Howard and Fayette, remembers that the Thompson's crowd was peppered with show-biz types who were doing three-a-day at the Hippodrome Theatre around the corner on Eutaw Street. Flitt remembers seeing the likes of Milton Berle, John Hodiak and Xavier Cugat eating at Thompson's. "People only ate at Thompson's because it was open; otherwise nobody would eat there," Flitt says. "The food was lousy." Still, even at those odd hours, there was often a line waiting to get in.

So your next bet would be Horn and Horn's between Guilford and Holliday. Here, eating your pancakes or chicken biscuits, you would find yourself in a Runyonesque crowd of City Hall types, racetrack touts, and strippers from The Block discussing world affairs with their managers.

So, with all due respect for the *Sun Magazine* writers, Glimpses has a question. Let's say we've sampled the best you have offered us and it's all very, very good just as you said it would be. Here it is 2 o'clock of any morning in this classy Baltimore Renaissance. Now what? Where we gonna go now? Thompson's, Horn's, and Nates and Leon's are closed.

HORN
AND HORN'S

AFTER YEARS of subway construction had nearly shut it down, Baltimore Street was reopened in the summer of 1983 with a celebration near the Charles Center Metro Station area. There were rousing speeches, marching music, and cheering crowds. But to old Baltimore-streeters who loved the street through the 1960's and '70's, something, and some people, were missing from the scene.

The something was Horn and Horn's Restaurant, and the some people were Horn's famous—and infamous—clientele.

Horn and Horn's was an improbable restaurant, conference center, all-night hangout and city headquarters at 304 East Baltimore Street, and was the area's soul, too—what Times Square was to Old Broadway. Not only was it the oldest restaurant still doing business in Baltimore (dating back well before the turn of the century), and not only was it the only restaurant to stay open all night long, but it was the only restaurant where Baltimore's rich and poor and winners and losers—judges and pimps, merchant princes and numbers writers, fashion executives and stripteasers, mayors and governors and City Hall types—all sat down next to each other and shared time and space at the ancient tables and counters.

King of the place was an aging and dexterous counterman named Kelly Raines. He had lightning-fast hands and an astonishing memory, so he never forgot your name and your face, or the way you liked your eggs.

It was this special mix of urban characters and urban ideas; of varied and sometimes outrageous dress and manners and conversation; of chicken biscuits and the famous Red Ball Special (corned beef, cabbage, potato, coffee—35 cents); of a long, complicated order given to a waitress who never wrote down a word, but who delivered it, letter-perfect, to your table—it was of all this going on at the same time that made Horn and Horn's an institution that, in turn, helped make the Baltimore Street of those days an institution.

On the morning of January 25, 1977 a "closed" sign was posted in the window of Horn and Horn's. Out on the cold sidewalk, the mourners—the guys and dolls and the politicians, the high rollers and the button-down bankers—read it reflectively. A reporter on the scene overheard one nattily dressed sports type ask a similarly dressed friend, "My God, where we gonna go now?"

Which explains why not everybody was at those ceremonies up there at the subway station area. Some old Horn and Horners had gotten word that Baltimore Street was reopening, so they just naturally assumed that Horn and Horn's was, too. And so at that very time these incorrigibles were out on the sidewalk before 304 East Baltimore Street (it's now a Wendy's) waiting to get into Horn and Horn's. That's what comes of eating too many of Kelly Raines' chicken biscuits.

THE ARTIST
LEFT OUT

T HE RECENT EXPANSION and renovation of the Baltimore Museum of Art has provided a handsome setting for the works of such famous artists as Cezanne, Gauguin and Matisse. But not included in the museum's collection is the work of one famous Baltimore artist, and considering the importance of the "Grand Opening Occasion," it should have been. After all, her career had all the elements of a local-girl-makes-good story.

She had grown up in poverty (literally at the animal level) in Liberia before moving to Baltimore, where her career as an artist and a media celebrity began and ended. She and her art were to be seen on national television (the Garry Moore Show) and her colorful abstract paintings were to hang in galleries at home and abroad as far away as Australia. Reuters News Service called her "a painter of genius."

The artist and subject of all this fame was a chimpanzee named Betsey, who lived, without apology, at the Baltimore Zoo. Betsey's art career was the brainchild of zoo director Arthur Watson, who insisted through the entire caper that Betsey's abstract paintings were "a major contribution to art." Betsey was, Watson insisted, not only expert but prolific. "She would turn out four or five saleable paintings in half an hour."

Betsey's art career started by chance one afternoon at the zoo. Watson recalls, "She was watching Dr. Tom (another chimp) trying to paint. I was experimenting, looking to see what a chimpanzee might turn out by way of fingerpainting. Dr. Tom wasn't interested. Suddenly Betsey grabbed the magenta jar and began to eat the paint. She apparently liked it, because then she ate the chrome yellow."

Then, without Watson's coaxing, Betsey began smearing her finger around some of the other colors, and a star—and an art career—was born.

Betsey died February 10, 1960, and maybe it's a good thing she wasn't around for the gala opening of the expanded museum. Had she been, artist that she was, she no doubt would have taken in the showing. That experience would have carried with it the danger that she could have seen some delicious-looking Cezanne, Gauguin or Matisse (heavy on the magenta and chrome yellow) and, so tempted, might have leaped out of the crowd—and eaten it right off the wall.

THE LAST
GREAT ORATOR

BALTIMORE POLITICAL CANDIDATES debating today have an easier time of it than did those candidates in the 1940's, '50's and '60's who found themselves up against that most formidable of political orators, Theodore Roosevelt McKeldin.

Everybody knows where McKeldin came from (South Baltimore) but nobody knows where that absolutely charming delivery of his came from. "It was part Irish, part Scotch, part English," Gerald Johnson, the late noted Baltimore journalist and author, once remarked, "but no part Baltimore. He created it and perfected it on the streets of South Baltimore and on debating teams in school, and then on the political circuit, stumping for his old boss, Mayor William F. Broening. He would debate anyone. He once debated an antagonist while standing in a garbage truck."

A Republican liberal in a heavily Democratic city and state, he talked his way into two terms as mayor and two terms as governor. And why was he a Republican? A famous McKeldin speech explains. "I'm a Republican because my grandfather was," and here his voice would rise sonorously. "He came from Scotland and saw people enslaved because they were not his color. He enlisted in the Union Army. He was killed in the Battle of the Monocacy, fighting under General Wallace, and was buried at Antietam. That made my father a Republican and I'm his son and that made me a Republican!" Pure McKeldinese.

He used to say that he got started in politics by talking. "I was at a meeting once and the guest speaker didn't show. The chairman asked me if I would be the speaker that night. So I got up and told a few stories and sat down. The chairman turned to me and asked, 'You got any more of those?' I got up and talked for another hour and 18 minutes."

Perhaps the most widely heard of McKeldin's orations was the speech he gave at the Republican National Convention in Chicago in 1952 when he nominated Eisenhower for President. Here is the end of that speech—spellbinding, spreadeagle,

vintage McKeldin:

"It is no distraction from the honor and glory of our first president to say of this man in our generation what Lighthorse Harry Lee said of the immortal George Washington. He is first in war, first in peace, and first in the hearts of his countrymen. It is with grea-a-a-t pri-i-i-de that I place before this convention as President of the United States, the name of DWIGHT . . . DAVID . . . EISENHOW-W-W-E-R-R-R-R!"

Roaring, crashing, thunderous applause! Political candidates debating today, skillful though they may be, no longer need fear such intimidating competition. Alas, the inimitable Teddy McKeldin is dead.

EAST NORTH AVENUE; HUH?

COLD SPRING LANE used to be Kate Avenue and up until the 1920's was the city's northern boundary. It was never, as you might think, called Boundary Avenue—that's in East Baltimore.

High Street meets Low Street—what's left of both of them, anyway. When the Orleans Street Viaduct opened in 1926 it was to be known as the Bath Street Viaduct, but the citizenry never got the word. *The Sun* tried to straighten things out: "It is now and always will be the Bath Street Viaduct, and that is what you had better ask to be directed to if you want to find it." Nobody listened. "Orleans Street Viaduct" it is and always has been.

In South Baltimore there's a West Street and an East West Street. Saint Paul Street, which now runs south, used to run north. The main north-south streets in the center of the city were reversed at 2 A.M. on the wild morning of July 8, 1954 by Traffic Commissioner Henry Barnes.

There's a Hendler Lane named after Hendler's Ice Cream (the company's founder lived adjacent to the Lane) and a Horseradish Court, named after Tulkoff's you-know-what. There is no Beer Street, but believe it or not there's a Crab Court over near Patterson Park. Edgar Allan Poe's house is *not* on Poe Avenue; it's on Amity Street.

There's a York Road, an Old York Road and a *New* York Road—and there's a Charles Street, a Charles Street Avenue, and a Charles Street Avenue Extended. Crazy.

Redwood Street used to be German Street, but only after it was Lovely Lane. If that surprises you, remember that only 20 years ago, Fells Point was known as Foot-of-Broadway.

To get to Bel Air (two words) you have to take Belair (one word) Road, and nobody knows Bel Air becomes Belair at the city line.

Although East Street does run easterly; West street, westerly; and South Street, southerly; North Avenue runs east and west. That is why there is an East North Avenue and a West North Avenue. It figures.

Monument Street runs one way west from Saint Paul, two ways for two blocks to Guilford, and then so-help-me it runs one way east!

A visitor might look for Rome Avenue to be in Little Italy. It isn't. And you would think a street with a magisterial name like "President Street" would be a flag-draped boulevard with a wide median strip leading into City Hall or something. It is no such thing. It is a tiny run-down cobblestone street winding unobtrusively around (you guessed it) Little Italy.

People who move to Baltimore will tell you that it's a great town and they love it, but some things about it are confusing. We understand.

SELLING OFF
OUR CITY

THE SELLING OFF OF BALTIMORE *(in our time, more or less). Being a brief history of how locally owned Baltimore businesses have been sold to (horrors!) out-of-town interests*

It was Jacob Epstein, millionaire Baltimore merchant, who started it all when in 1929 he sold his Baltimore Bargain House to Butler Brothers of Chicago. The price was around $30 million (1929 dollars). It was the fourth largest business of its kind in America, and the building it occupied at the northwest corner of Baltimore at Liberty across from the Civic Center still stands.

The decade that followed was one that led up to World War II and Baltimore businesses were so busy they had no time to think of selling out, so there was little or none of it during that time. But right after WWII, Epstein's precedent was there to follow.

Without regard to industry or chronology, and with apologies for omissions ("due to space limitations"), here's what happened: Hochschild Kohn's sold out to Supermarkets General; Commercial Credit to Control Data; Hendler's Ice Cream to Borden's; Meadow Gold to Beatrice Foods. Greif sold to Genesco; Schoeneman to Cluett Peabody; Isaac Hamburger to Van Heusen; Pemco to Glidden; Maryland Casualty to American General; and Title Guarantee also to American General. Legg sold to Mason; Stein Brothers to Bache; Read's ("Run Right to...") to Rite Aid; Gino's to Marriott; Baltimore Luggage to Sonnenbend; Head Ski to AMF; J.H. Filbert to Central Soya; Western Maryland Railroad and the B & O to Chessie (and Chessie was then absorbed into CSX); Joseph Bank to Quaker Oats. And on and on.

Epstein started his business in a small room on Barre Street, and he lived to see it expand into what was then one of the most imposing buildings in all of downtown. In the years since Epstein sold his business, many other old Baltimore businesses have been sold. Some retain their names, others have seen the name gone forever from the scene. But through it all, Epstein's building still stands, a modest 12-story souvenir of where it all began; a little something of old Baltimore business to hold onto, as the names in the new Baltimore change furiously all around it.

FERTILIZER
IN THE AIR

"TWO MORE COMPANIES plan to enter the week-long Chesapeake Cruise business next year," a story in *The Evening Sun* reports, and goes on to say that these two new cruise ship companies, Windsor of St. Louis and Coast-wise of Hyannis, Mass., will compete with the already-in-business American Cruise Lines of Connecticut. "All three," says the story, "have similar itineraries, including stops at Annapolis, Crisfield and Yorktown, Va."

The announcement may well come off to Baltimoreans as joyous news—fulfilling, as it were, the promise of the burgeoning Baltimore Renaissance and bringing back the golden era of the down-the-bay cruise ships. But even if the number of cruises down the bay and out of Baltimore gets up to five in the next five years, it will still be less than there were 30 or 40 years ago, before anybody ever heard of a Renaissance.

The Old Bay Line's *City of Norfolk* made overnight cruises to Norfolk and Richmond, racing its competitor, the Chesapeake Line. The Merchants and Miners' ships steamed north to Philadelphia and Boston, and south to Miami and Jacksonville, among other ports-of-call. The Baltimore Mail Steamship line ran cruises to Le Havre, France. The *Smokey Joe* ferryboats cruised to Philadelphia. And of course there were countless cruises to the Eastern Shore and daily excursions to Tolchester and Betterton and Fort Smallwood and Fairview Beach.

The three new cruise lines promise days of sunshine and tranquility, and nights of moonlight and romance. But of course, so did those earlier cruises. The difference between down-the-bay cruises then and now will be noticed when the ships return home and enter the Inner Harbor.

Today, passengers will perceive the Inner Harbor coming into view as a light show sparkling in the night, the Aquarium and Harborplace and the Science Center creating a velvet-lined jewel box to contain it all. Back then, the view was simpler: the dimly lit silhouette of the Maryland National Bank Building and the cupolas of the rickety old Bay Line piers.

Most distinctively, however, passengers were greeted by an aroma they would never forget, and that told them they were home in Baltimore, which was at the time one of the world's leading producers of fertilizer. Such giant companies as Baugh, Miller, and Dietrich & Summers sent out regularly into the summer night that welcome-home odor of ground bone, manure, guano and dried fish.

If we're going to bring back the era of the down-the-bay cruise ships, we're going to have to bring back, too, that peculiar Baltimore odor of fertilizer that was inseparable from the era, and characterized it. Re-creating that odor in the Inner Harbor to give authenticity to the new and growing cruise ship business in Baltimore—now *there's* one for Jim Rouse!

THE TOURISTS'
REAL BALTIMORE

BALTIMORE TOURISM is going big time—there are more buses bringing in the tourists than ever before, and there is now a tie-in to British tourism, linking Baltimore to other East Coast cities along the tourist trail. *Glimpses* leaves to the professionals which of the attractions to include in any given tour of Baltimore, but we do feel the need to offer Our Very Own Alternative Tour of Baltimore. Here goes.

Joe Poodles Pool Hall. In a converted row house deep in the shadows of the Canton canneries that overwhelm it on all sides, is one of Baltimore's best and least-known museums—and you thought it was only a pool parlor! On the walls is the largest collection of boxing pictures (local and national) in the city. It's a gritty, sweaty Baltimore no tourists' tour will get you to. Dress casually.

The Roland Park Water Tower. Totally useless and totally ugly—you must see it. It was built in 1904 and has had little use since. It once held 200,000 gallons of water. Now it holds nothing but memories—and 54 steps leading to the top. Bring your camera.

The Four Corners of High and Fawn Streets in Little Italy. It only looks like nothing's going on here, but it's the center of street life in Baltimore—and everything is going on here. More celebrities appear on these four corners than in any posh restaurant in Baltimore. Open all night, no admission charge.

Fort Carroll. You can't get there from here or anyplace else, except by small boat. The ancient ruin, built in 1832 by Robert E. Lee himself, sits sullen and brooding in the main channel of the Patapsco, just south of the Francis Scott Key Bridge. It was supposed to be "the strong outerline of defense for the city" but it was never that or anything else save a spooky haven for seagulls and swallows, and a vague dream of planners that it might one day be a gambling casino. Barren and wholly uninviting. Stick close to your guide.

Galley in the Alley Delicatessen in Pikesville. A bagel-and-lox Sunday morning gathering place, but you probably couldn't get in even if you tried, and if you did you probably couldn't get served. The place is that jammed. Men come early and stay late and table hop and in the interchange settle such grave issues as the outcome of the fifth at Pimlico. Reservations? Hah!

A tour like this, with its secret promise to take you places you couldn't get to by yourself, places denied the ordinary citizen, places that let you talk about Baltimore with the self-confidence of an insider—a tour like this will fill up fast.

Better talk to your travel agent soon!

CIVIC CENTER'S HISTORY

THE HISTORY of the Civic Center actually has seven chapters. Six are complete and one is incomplete because now the Blast want to buy the place. That's funny, and if you don't think so, ask former Mayor Tommy D'Alesandro, Jr. But first, read on.

CHAPTER ONE: Just after World War II a company headed by aircraft tycoon Glenn L. Martin, responding to citizen interest in a Baltimore civic center, proposes a stadium with an air-supported roof. He is called a "crazy dreamer" and all that happens is that the city improves Municipal Stadium.

CHAPTER TWO: Now the Greater Baltimore Committee joins the quest, calling for private financing of a center. That hope dies aborning, and the committee lays the financing problem on Mayor D'Alesandro (The Elder). He promptly tosses it to the state, which gets a $6 million civic center loan on the ballot. The voters, in a careless mood they are to regret, approve it without even knowing where the center is to be built. That inattention to detail is to create one of the stormiest chapters in the political history of the city.

CHAPTER THREE: Studies suggest more than 30 locations, including Mt. Royal Station, Pimlico Race Track, Fort Carroll, City Hospitals, Druid Hill Park, Carlin's Park, Lake Clifton—and over (on stilts, as it were) the Jones Falls Expressway. The GBC, after a careful study of the facts, comes in with its final recommendation—Carlin's Park. Downtown interests raise hell, claiming that putting the center "all the way out in the country" (this is Park Circle, mind you) will take business away from downtown. They suggest Sam Smith Park (now Harborplace).

CHAPTER FOUR: In one of the hottest Augusts on record, 1957, in one of the most bizarre acts in the bizarre history of Baltimore politics, Tommy drops a bombshell. He announces that he has decided that the civic center will be built on the edge of Druid

Hill Park Lake. The citizenry screams. Sam Hammerman of the Park Board says the proposal will "rape this beautiful park." Tommy, defiant, calls a special session of the City Council. Hyman Pressman—then an unofficial civic gadfly—takes the city to court, and ultimately the council's approval of the mayor's proposal is ruled illegal.

CHAPTER FIVE: An exhausted electorate and a mayor out of patience finally agree (June 4, 1958) on Hopkins Place, a location that wasn't one of the sites originally proposed.

CHAPTER SIX: The Civic Center is dedicated March 30, 1963. Mayor J. Harold Grady presides over the dedication, and former Mayor Tommy D'Alesandro does not attend.

CHAPTER SEVEN: July, 1983, and the word is out that the Baltimore Blast want to buy the Civic Center. We don't know how this chapter will end, but if we were to ask old Tommy D'Alesandro, we can anticipate his answer:

"They can have it."

SAM'S
PARKING LEGACY

THIS IS THE STORY of how Baltimore got parking meters, and why General Sam Smith, whose statue now sits atop Federal Hill and who is credited with winning the Battle of the Parking Meters in Baltimore, is also discredited for losing the Battle of the Parking Meters (and, in the end, gets the last laugh).

The debate in the City Council on the April evenings of 1955 was particularly intense. At issue was whether the city should install parking meters—there were none in Baltimore—but the debate would turn on whether the city should install meters in the newly created Sam Smith Park. A vote for meters in Sam Smith Park was, in fact, a vote to install meters all over Baltimore.

The park would accommodate 350 parking spaces in an area created by widening Light Street eastward to the harbor just after the old piers and warehouses were torn down. The centerpiece of the park was to be the statue of the old general himself. It was to be placed in a commanding position at the corner of Light and Pratt. The statue was in Wyman Park at the time, and though the city presented careful plans for removing it, the 29th Division Organization fought the idea—to a standstill.

In the City Council debate, traffic Commissioner Henry Barnes rose to make the point that other cities were realizing revenues from parking meters, and Baltimore should, too. Though the opposition, which was considerable, called the meter idea "socialistic," the vote was for installing the meters.

As planned, some weeks later the city finally moved the general (over loud protests) to Sam Smith Park, where he presided over the city's very first metered parking lot. In 1970 the city closed the park to make way for the Inner Harbor development, and the general was moved again—this time to Federal Hill. There he stands comfortably, staring down with what must be satisfaction.

He knows that if they hadn't created a Sam Smith Park, if they hadn't dragged his good name through the mud, setting up the perfect door-opener for what was to be the parking metering of Baltimore, maybe there wouldn't be all those people stuffing all those coins into all those meters. Serves them right, he must be thinking, for not letting an old general rest in peace.

THE END OF LEXINGTON STREET

I T WAS SPRING, 1961. The tulips in Preston Gardens along St. Paul Street had burst into flaming bloom. Advertisements had begun to appear for the Bay Belle moonlight excursions. But for the one block of Lexington Street between Charles and Liberty it had been a long and weary winter of discontent.

The word was out about this wondrous street of the Century Theater (where Harvey Hammond played the mighty Wurlitzer organ and got you to sing along and follow the bouncing ball) and the Valencia Theater ("clouds" moved and "stars" twinkled in its ceiling-sky). The city was buying up all the property on the street to make way for Charles Center.

Many of the familiar retailers—Whelan's, Goldenberg's, Baltimore Lunch—had already moved out. Now, in the windows of the stores that were left, signs told passers-by that Ritz Camera, Huyler's Fountain Shop and Planter's Peanuts were moving or would close. O'Neill's, once Baltimore's famous department store emporium of fine linens, was now a dark shell.

Along the narrow, windswept sidewalks where vendors had once sold roasted chestnuts, shopping bags and improbable tiny packets of lavender, the merchandising "gypsies" had taken over—vultures hovering over the dying, waiting for the kill. "Folding Binoculars $1.88" and "Men's Watches $3.57."

Streetcars had been rerouted to Saratoga Street. A blind beggar had made the corner of Lexington and Little Sharp streets his favorite spot over these last months of the street's fading glory. Seated on a low stool in the warming sun, he read his braille Bible and talked cheerfully. He did a fine business, sensing that the mood of impending loss would make pedestrians generous.

Stagnation had turned to decay, decay to blight. But the patient, although desperately ill, would not die. "It's like doing business in Virginia City," one merchant said, "after the Comstock Lode gave out."

Then suddenly and mercifully, in midmorning of June 28, 1961, the city put up

barricades at both ends of this Lexington Street block. It was all over. The wrecking ball was not far behind. Now, nothing remains.

Gone the Century and the sound of Harvey Hammond; and the Valencia with its Land-of-Oz ceiling; and Huyler's and Planter's Peanuts and Maron's and the vendors selling chestnuts and shopping bags and lavender.

But, if you are a Baltimorean who remembers this once-and-famous block and you miss it badly enough, then on spring days when your mood is right, you can still catch—faint and far away—the lovely aroma of lavender.

SHOPS THAT
MISSED THE TRAIN

WHEN THE DOWNTOWN subway stations opened in the late summer of 1983, the areas around them swarmed with people—coming and going, shopping and waiting. Those swollen crowds, unknown in these parts of downtown since the 1950's, gave businesses in the vicinity of the stations a big boost. Alas, a lot of the businessmen who should be around today to enjoy the long-awaited boom are not. Their timing was off, and that's too bad.

Wouldn't all those clothing stores, men's and women's—Warner's and Cowan's and Jos. Schloss and K. Katz and Schleisner's and Maison Annette and Mildred Davis—have been sitting pretty if only they had stayed around longer?

And wouldn't the Hub (northeast corner of Charles and Baltimore, where the W.R. Grace Building is today) have done a land-office business? We can see those ads now: "Subway Riders' Specials, One half off today only!"

That famous old movie palace, the Stanley, had it stayed open until today, would find itself only a few blocks from the Lexington Market Station, and what a business it would be doing!

And speaking of palaces, what about the Palace Theater? (Fayette between Eutaw and Howard)? It opened as the Palace in 1913, became a garage in 1937, and in 1947 became a theater again, the Town.

And all those restaurants—the old pre-Hilton Miller Brothers and Baum's and Johnson's Mecca and the old Oyster Bay—that have closed down; a couple more years of holding on and they wouldn't have needed all those reviews to bring in their customers. The subway would have done that in large numbers.

Waiting would have saved the night clubs—the Picadilly and the Spanish Villa (atop the Southern Hotel) and the Copa and the Chesapeake Lounge of the Hotel Emerson. They'd all be playing to standing-room-only crowds!

And the famous specialty stores downtown—oh, if they had only hung in there! Malcolm's House and Garden Shop (500 block N. Charles) and Thomas and Thompson's Drug store (southeast corner, Baltimore & Light) and Hopper McGaw (Charles at Mulberry), Baltimore's fine food store.

Well, the crowds that disgorge from the busy subway stations by the thousands every day will not be patronizing these fine old establishments which seem to have been in the wrong place at the wrong time. Put another way, by moving or closing down when they did, they missed the boat. Or more accurately, the train.

LEGAL
SLOT MACHINES

I T IS A WARM spring night in April of 1960. Cars are bumper-to-bumper heading north over the one-lane bridge that crosses the Potomac, leading to Maryland Highway 301 into Charles County. At that same time, heading south down 301 from Baltimore and points north, another crowded lane of traffic is moving.

A stranger to these parts might wonder where all those cars are headed in such a hurry, and if you follow them for a few more miles and a few more minutes, you'll see they are, as the 1960 expression runs, "hitting Highway 301" along that 20-mile stretch from Waldorf to the Potomac River Bridge. In these pre-Atlantic City days there are only two places in all America that have legal slot machines paying off in cash. One is Nevada; the other, right here in the four counties that make up Southern Maryland—Anne Arundel, Charles, St. Mary's, Calvert.

More than 200 gambling spots do business along this road, in grimy little roadside restaurants, bars, taverns and filling stations. One of them on this evening in April 1960 is Delbert Connor's tavern. The changemaker, standing in the doorway, is saying to a reporter, "Stick around. There'll be 500 people jamming this place in a few minutes. You won't be able to find a machine not being used."

He turns out to be right. The crowds swarm in; people take their positions before the machines. Many of them are grey-haired and elderly, and they will stand (and some in chairs will sit) for hours, watching the spinning fruit and bars, now and then collecting a few coins as scant reward for their faith. One hefty country-woman type is busy playing three slots at one time while her 5-year-old son and 9-year-old daughter wait restlessly beside her. A couple from Washington says they come here three nights a week. "It's good entertainment," the lady says, though obviously less than entertained when a losing combination of plum, cherry and bar spring into place underneath the glass.

One lady is wearing a golf glove and cranking the handle of the "slot" with a steady rhythm. "I come up from Richmond four times a week. I always play this one machine. I can't leave now, this one's about due."

This one's about due—someone is no doubt saying that standing in front of a "slot" in a lush and spangled casino in Atlantic City as you read this, but a little old grey-haired lady wearing a golf glove was saying it 20 years ago, while facing a "slot" in a bare, spare joint along Highway 301 in southern Maryland, when—believe it or not—little old Waldorf was America's Atlantic City.

ARTIE SHAW, BRENT GUNTS
AND THE DIXIE

ARTIE SHAW FORMS NEW BAND.
The *New York Times*, December 19, 1983

It is Wednesday night, April 10, 1940 at the Dixie Ballroom in Gwynn Oak Park. The Dixie was a cavernous dance pavilion (torn down in the 1960's) that played host to big bands that were one-night-standing across America in those days. It is 11:15 on this particular night and at the moment there is a hush over the place. The music and dancing have stopped and all eyes are fixed on an announcer on the bandstand in front of a WFBR microphone. He has his hand up, motioning for quiet. He gets it and then in his best announcer's voice says, to the crowd and into the mike, "From the Dixie Ballroom here in beautiful Gwynn Oak Park we're bringing you the swing music of Artie Shaw and his big band. Artie and the boys are going to get things started with 'Begin the Beguine.' Take it, Mr. Artie Shaw . . ."

The announcer was Brent Gunts, who has been part of Baltimore broadcasting for 50 years. His was one of the voices, Artie Shaw's was one of the bands, and the Dixie Ballroom one of the ballroom dancehalls you could tune in on your old Philco radio in 1940—if you stayed up as late as 11:15.

Others you could catch were Don Bestor from the Charles Room of the Belvedere; Lou Becker from the Southern Hotel; Bob Iula from the Keith's Roof.

"I remember announcing from the Dixie Ballroom," Brent Gunts recalled recently. "Tommy Dorsey, Hudson DeLange, Glenn Miller. We'd go on the air at 11:15 and off at 11:45. Then the stations would pick up the big bands from the Glen Island Casino, the Savoy Ballroom, the Hotel Pennsylvania, all up in the New Jersey-New York area. And it was all straight, uninterrupted music. There were no commercials because it was thought there probably were not a lot of people listening. So the time wasn't commercially valuable."

That same story announcing Artie Shaw's return also announced that he staged that return "at the newly restored Glen Island Casino in New Rochelle, N.Y." In all of this there's a mad, marvelous dreamy idea for minds such as ours.

Artie Shaw is back. Brent Gunts is still in town. WFBR is very much with us. All we have to do now is rebuild the Dixie Ballroom and then re-stage that whole memorable evening of April 10, 1940. We give the microphone back to Brent Gunts and turn him loose. Listen: "From the Dixie Ballroom here in beautiful Gwynn Oak Park, we bring you the swing music of Artie Shaw . . ."

Brent said of big band broadcasting in the old days, "There probably were not a lot of people listening." *Glimpses*, defiant, speaks for its readers. Put that evening together one more time and try us.

EDITOR'S NOTE: I spent a few evenings at the Dixie, and I remember most vividly a detail Gil has omitted: no gentleman was admitted without a tie on. If you walked in without a tie, the management of the Dixie furnished you with a greasy chunk of rep to knot about your neck. It wasn't pretty, but by God, you knew the Dixie insisted on some standards.

NEW YEAR'S EVE
ON THE BLOCK

DEAR DIARY. Well, here it is, my first entry of the New Year, Jan. 1, 1953. I guess I ought to tell you what we did last night, New Year's Eve—if I can remember.

We decided to do the Block, or it decided to do us, I'm not sure. Anyway, we started out by taking in the show at the Gayety. "Lovely Lotus DuBois" was the featured stripper, but how we missed Georgia Southern, Patti Waggin, Ann Corio! We got out about 11:00 and found the streets jammed with people.

We were practically pushed into Blaze Starr's 2 O'Clock Club, but people were lined up four and five deep along the runway and bar, so we couldn't see a thing. But we did hear that Blaze herself was the featured stripper that night. Oh, well.

We left and headed toward Bettye Mills' Stork Club and found Bettye herself there, meeting and greeting. She welcomed us in and said, "Enjoy the show," and although we could hear all that bump-and-grind music, we couldn't see a thing, the place was so packed.

Somebody suggested the Oasis. We got in but we couldn't see a thing there either—even so, we could hear MC Willie Grey going through his familiar routine: "Here they are, ladies and gentlemen, presenting the world's worst show and these lovely, lovely ladies taking the night off from the House of the Good Shepherd."

The crowd was too much for us so we left and hit, one right after the other, the Circus, the Florida Cafe, the K-9 Club, the Troc—we must have been in every one of the eight clubs between Holliday Street and Market Place. Mobbed.

By this time it was four in the morning, so we decided to get something to eat. A couple of us chose Horn & Horn's, and the rest drove up to Nates and Leon's on North Avenue. From the crowd and the lights and the noise and the traffic, you'd have thought it was a circus at noon. I ordered my usual Number 3—corned beef and cole slaw on rye, with coffee and cheesecake. By this time it was getting on to daylight, which was time to sing Auld Lang Syne to the Block, and to 1952, and to call it a

night, or a year.

Author's Note: Friend, if in your merrymaking this New Year's Eve, you decide to try and see Blaze Starr performing, or Willie Grey at the Oasis MC'ing, or to take in the K-9 Club, the Troc, Kaye's, the Miami, the Florida, or the Circus Bar—believe me, you can't do it, they are all gone. And if you don't believe me and you still have the urge, promise me you'll call a cab or have a friend drive you home. Explain that you've been imbibing too much Baltimore nostalgia. They'll understand. Happy New Year.

THE GREAT
1959 PRIMARY

DID YOU VOTE in the Baltimore Mayoral Primary of 1959? If you did, you helped make Baltimore history, and you should be recognized for it—which we'll get around to in a minute.

That election pitted Tommy D'Alesandro, Jr. (seeking his fourth term amid charges that he had become the "prisoner of Jack Pollack") against J. Harold Grady ("He's the darling of the reformers!").

Grady ran on the "3-G" ticket with R. Walter Graham and Philip Goodman, and had the support of *The Sun* and *The Evening Sun.*

It was a heated, bitter and hard-fought campaign, but it excited little public interest until just a few weeks before the election when Governor Tawes appointed members of the Pollack-D'Alesandro organization to 11 of the top 14 state jobs in Baltimore. That raised the pitch of the battle.

By Election Day nobody would call the election, it was that uncertain. The day (March 3) started with Grady voting at 6 A.M. at his Northwood polling place, and D'Alesandro across town and at about the same time stopping into St. Leo's Church in Little Italy to pray. (Later he would say, "I never pray for a political victory.")

By noon it was obvious to observers that something extraordinary was going on. A judge of elections called headquarters and put it this way: "I'll tell you what's going on," he said. "Voting's so heavy they're coming out of the walls." By 3 P.M. in one precinct 500 out of 700 registered voters had already cast ballots. Half an hour later, Charles Dorsey, president of the Elections Board increased his estimate of the vote to 40 percent. Then Chief Clerk Eugene Sokolow said, "The percentage is going to go through the roof."

At D'Alesandro headquarters the b'hoys said the vote was this heavy because the voters were "mad as hell at *The Sunpapers*" (for urging them to vote for Grady). At Grady headquarters they said the vote was so heavy because the people were tired of the machine.

At 7 P.M. it was over and at 8:06 Tommy picked up the phone. "Harold, you've won. Congratulations!"

And then the figures began to come in—so big no one could believe them. 180,000 Democrats had voted, 54.2 percent of the vote, the largest number and the largest percentage ever in a Democratic primary—before or since.

If you didn't vote in that election you missed being counted in the record book. If you did vote, you helped make history, and *Glimpses* sends you its recognition: membership in the Order of the BWVDP59 (Baltimoreans Who Voted in Democratic Primary of 1959). It's something to tell your grandchildren about.

WAR ADMIRAL
VS. SEABISCUIT

I N VALLEY CLUBS and Highlandtown taverns, when they talk sports they talk about the big plays of the Colts and the Orioles, but because Baltimore was first a race-betting town, they talk especially about horses. Here is a favorite story:

At 8:30 on the damp morning of November 1, 1938, Jervis Spencer, Jr., chairman of the Maryland Racing Commission, stepped out onto the track at Pimlico and slowly walked the entire mile oval. When Spencer finally crossed the finish line 33 minutes later, he gave the racetrack's officials and the world the word: "This track," he said, "will be ready by post time. The race is on."

"The Race" was a rivalry that had been building for two years, between a Cinderella horse, Seabiscuit, the nation's undisputed handicap king, and War Admiral, the turf aristocrat that had won the Triple Crown.

Shortly after Spencer made his pronouncement the gates were thrown open and 40,000 people jammed the grandstand, clubhouse and infield. Tension mounted through the morning, and by post time the sun was shining, the crowd was on its feet and the horses—War Admiral the favorite—were on their walk-up start.

Seabiscuit broke suddenly with a tremendous burst of speed, moved ahead by a length, and the race was on. They ran indecisively for most of the way. Then, coming into the backstretch, War Admiral's nose showed in front. That's when George Woolf, Seabiscuit's jockey, slashed his mount with the whip and brought the horses head to head. Charlie Kurtsinger, who stated before the race that he had never had to ask War Admiral for his best, asked now. With all the power that had made him one of the country's leading riders, he drove War Admiral forward, begging for more.

But War Admiral could give no more. He had met a better horse. Seabiscuit drew away and won by four lengths. They still talk about that race, and some call it bigger than Unitas's touchdown bombs or Brooks' vacuum cleaner stops. For some, Baltimore will always be a racetrack town.

NORTH AVENUE'S
SPORTS CENTER

THE MERCHANTS in the North Avenue and Charles Street area have been looking for ideas to revitalize their once vibrant, lively community, close to the geographic center of the city. They have in mind a certain magical mix of shops and/or civic attractions that will bring back the people and the community's interest. Too bad this isn't 1955. They would not have had to look hard—or far. There it was, right in their own back yard, on North Avenue just east of Charles on what is now (naturally) a parking lot: the Sports Center.

The Sports Center was mostly an ice rink, but with a commodious lobby that, with its snack shop and booths and tables, was a popular gathering place for ice-show and hockey fans, and for their families and their dates and their friends. At least two hockey leagues played there. One was made up of teams representing local businesses (A.D. Anderson, Silber's Bakery, etc.) and the other, of high schools—McDonogh, Tome, Forest Park, City, Poly, Gilman, Loyola, Calvert Hall, Mt. St. Joseph.

There were also, believe it or not, two all-girl ice hockey teams that played each other regularly—the "Glamour Girls" and the "Spitfires".

Every Saturday beginning at 10 A.M. the place was open for public skating and on certain nights during the winter there were ice skating pageants, which brought to town the superstar skaters from America's best known skating clubs.

In the mid-1950's pressure was exerted to tear down the Center and put the land to other use. But Josh Cockey, then manager, announced bold plans not only to save it but to enlarge it. "We will build a brand new Sports Center," Cockey told the press. "And it will be on this very site, here at North and Charles. The rink will be on the second floor. There will be plenty of parking on the ground floor. Plans are being drafted right now."

But not much came of those plans. In the end, the Sports Center was torn down and the ice skaters and their cheering fans lay scattered about, rinkless (Carlin's had

closed only a few years earlier), and Baltimore's ice skaters fell upon years of hard times.

Gone now from North and Charles are all signs of hockey players and crowds milling about, waiting to get in the Sports Center. Gone, figure-eighters whirling in the color of the beams of light making multiple x-patterns on the milky-white surface of the ice. Gone, streetcars and automobiles, and vendors selling peanuts and pennants. Gone, the noise and the traffic and the life and the sounds of that long-ago innocent merriment.

Now the same community is looking for an attraction to liven up the place. Oh Josh Cockey! Where are you and your brand-new Sports Center, now that we need you?

THE FLAGPOLE
AND THE DOCTOR

O N THE MORNING of July 22, 1929, Dr. Samuel Shipley Glick, then a practicing pediatrician in Baltimore, took a phone call from a worried parent and, in so doing, became a part of local lore and legend.

The call was from a Mrs. McCruden. Her 13-year-old daughter, Ruth, Mrs. McCruden explained, was "sitting on top of a flagpole" in the backyard of a house at 5704 Ethelbert Avenue in Pimlico. Ruth was just getting over scarlet fever and Mrs. McCruden was concerned.

But to understand what Ruth was doing sitting on top of a "flagpole" in the first place you have to understand that in 1929 Baltimore was a national center for flagpole sitting. That reputation began in the late afternoon of July 19, 1929 when a 15-year-old boy named Avon ("Azey") Foreman climbed to the top of an 18-foot sapling in the rear of his Pimlico home and, on a special platform he had constructed, sat down. He promptly announced that he was going to stay up there until he had set a record no one could match.

Azey had been inspired by an ex-boxer named Shipwreck Kelly who had been going around the country sitting on flagpoles atop hotels as publicity stunts. Newspaper reports recounted Azey's effort, and in a matter of days he was world famous. Crowds by the thousands descended on the Foremans' modest backyard. Boys and girls, even adults throughout the nation began to compete with him. Which is why 13-year-old Ruth McCruden climbed up to Azey's perch, determined to share in his record stay, or perhaps go beyond it.

The situation moved Ruth's mother to call Dr. Glick to come out and try to persuade Ruth to come down. Fifty years later the doctor would recall the incident: "I arrived at the house and found that somebody had placed a ladder against the tree for me to go up where Ruth was. I climbed up and as best I could, I examined her. I found her in excellent health. As for persuading her to come down, Ruth would have none of it. She said she was feeling fine, and would stay at least as long as Azey did."

By now, daily reports of life atop the flagpole were being cabled worldwide. Mayor Broening paid Azey and Ruth a personal visit. Exactly 10 days, 10 hours and 10 minutes later on July 29, Ruth and Azey descended—to the cheers of more than 4,000 well-wishers.

Azey and Ruth were now like gunfighters; they had to be taken. Dozens of Baltimoreans began to flagpole-sit in the hope of knocking off Azey's record. During one week in 1929, Baltimore had no fewer than 20 flagpole sitters (17 boys, 3 girls), among them William Ruppert from Highlandtown (55 days), Willie Wentworth and Dorothy Saylor.

Half a century later Dr. Glick could still remember the call from Mrs. McCruden, the climb up the flagpole with his stethoscope, the examination of Ruth. And his diagnosis, after all these years?

"Flagpole sitting is good for your health!"

EDITOR'S NOTE: The sequel to this tall tale illustrates how often fate conspires to surprise and amuse us. Not a week after this column appeared in The Evening Sun, *our mutual friend Gilbert was attending a banquet at one of our local lavish catering palaces, when who should appear at his table but Dr. Samuel Shipley Glick himself. "I have to tell you," said the good Doctor, "that I have never in my life been so famous as I have been this week. Everyone I ever met must have read that article!" Gil was pleased, of course, at this additional piece of evidence that Baltimore loves* Glimpses *but not half so pleased as Dr. Glick, who positively glowed at his new-found celebrity status.*

THE SAFETY
(WET) ZONE

THE ATTRACTIONS of the new subway are mind-boggling—the speed, the comfort, the economy. But to old Baltimoreans with a lifetime history of riding the streetcars and later the buses, the most attractive feature of the subway system is the subway station itself. A real, honest-to-God station, warm in the winter, cool in the summer, out of the weather and providing a way to wait far removed from the screech and the scream of automobiles streaking by.

Though the MTA has provided glass-and-aluminum shelters built well back from the street at selected stops around the city, that amenity has come only in the last 10 years or so. Twenty years ago there were no such shelters. When it rained, you got wet; when it snowed, you got white. Always—save for a few wooden three-sided shacks in Ellicott City, Manhattan Loop, Roland Park, Halethorpe, and Glyndon—you waited for the streetcar out in the weather. Worse, out in the middle of the street.

Streetcars, obviously, could not veer to the curb as buses do, so you walked out to meet them in the middle where the tracks usually were. And out there, your only protection from the autos and trucks passing on either side were "safety-zone" markers. A marker's base was a four-foot chunk of concrete. Built-in lead pipes extended upward into them about 8 feet. The whole arrangement was painted black and yellow. Although these safety-zone markers (or pylons) were highly visible and well-lit, automobiles wrapped themselves around those markers quite regularly.

Safety-zone markers were removed along with streetcar tracks in the '50's and '60's to make way for "progress" in the form of buses, which pull up to the curb to meet you as you emerge from the safety of the aluminum-and-glass shelter.

Old streetcar and bus riders, veterans of long, dark and numbing waits in all weather, and of fearful times huddled against the life-side of the safety-zone markers and the fragile glass of the bus shelters, can now enjoy some comfort. Just waiting in the station will make the ride worth the fare.

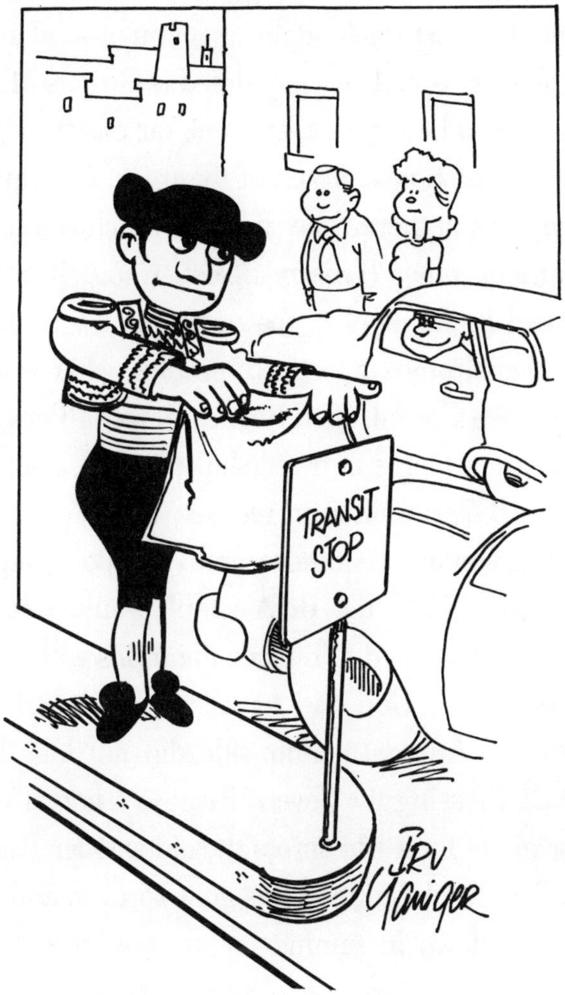
TRANSIT STOP
IRV Yaniger

RATTLE AND ROLL
ON THE B&A

NOW THAT THE SUBWAY is running to Reisterstown Road Plaza, there is talk about where the next track ought to go. Suggested are the Inner Harbor and Johns Hopkins Hospital; already slated is Owings Mills.

But *Glimpses* has a better idea, and one far easier to get going with, too: pick up the old B&A run to Annapolis. Much of the track, and the remains of the old bridge across the Severn are still there. The railroad, which ran out of three separate Baltimore stations at various times (Liberty Street, Camden Station, Howard and Lombard) to Bladen Street in Annapolis, was notorious as the roughest, rattlingest interurban in America. The trip took a long 55 minutes, what with no fewer than 30 stops at such places as English Consul, Glen Burnie, Severna Park.

The road's beginnings are a tangle of ownership changes, and much of its history, going all the way back to 1837, is written in red ink. It started as the Annapolis and Elkridge, became the Washington, Baltimore and Annapolis, and finally the Baltimore and Annapolis. In the 1940's the B&A simply could not make money as a railroad, and the management decided to replace the trains with buses.

Cries of anguish went up as if God had replaced Noah's Ark with a canoe. The changing leaves of the Anne Arundel countryside did not look the same from the windows of a speeding bus. Crossing the Severn River in a line of fuming automobiles was not a civilized replacement for a trip across the old wooden trestle by train.

But it was all too late. The B&A Railroad was gone forever, and with it the memory of windows invariably stuck down in summer or up in winter, of jerky rides with a mail-train pattern of starts and stops, of comic peep-peeps at every arrival and departure.

Oldtimers tell this one story, apocryphal or not, about the last day of the old B&A; Lady goes to ticket window, asks for a first-class ticket. Agent laughs; says, "Lady, guess you haven't ridden this train before." Lady, annoyed, says, "No, young man, have you?" "No ma'am," agent guffaws. "Not since they took the egg stoves out of

the aisles." That kind of a train.

Granted, running the subway along the tracks of the old B&A may not be the best use of the taxpayers' money. Granted, the run may not bring in a lot of fares. But it certainly ought to bring back a lot of memories.

THE LAST ROYAL BLUE

ABOUT A QUARTER TO FIVE in the afternoon of April 28, 1958, there was a sudden bustle of activity in Mount Royal Station, down in the grassy hollow where Mount Royal Avenue meets Cathedral Street. The activity was predictable: the famous B&O Royal Blue to New York was taking on passengers in response to the conductor's "All aboar-r-r-rd!" On this day, and because this trip was the last one the famous Royal Blue would ever make to New York (service would be discontinued after this run), the usual crowd had been swelled by railroad buffs and souvenir hunters.

It had been this very Royal Blue's arrivals and departures every day for 62 years that accounted for much of the railroading that really went on in Mount Royal Station. "Standing around doing nothing day after day," said a porter who once worked there, "used to get on my nerves."

From the moment it opened in 1896 with its Romanesque design and red tile roof right out of Hansel and Gretel, it was thought to be old-fashioned, and the place moved sleepily through the years at that pace and in that mood. The ambience in the waiting room was of a mountain lodge after dinner, and positively soporific. Fires burned in fireplaces at either end of the station. Art exhibits periodically turned the station into an art gallery.

Four rocking chairs made the whole place look like somebody's veranda. Once, in 1943, the chairs suddenly disappeared. Citizen outcry was so vociferous that management felt compelled to explain publicly that the chairs were only being repaired and would be returned soon. And indeed they were.

Outside, the slopes formed an amphitheatre, and crowds would gather in it for carnival-like celebrations. They cheered Cardinal Gibbons, Herbert Hoover, Woodrow Wilson, the Queen of Romania.

But by 1961 passenger trains stopped coming through Mount Royal altogether.

The rocking chairs disappeared, this time to no outcry whatever; celebrities neither arrived nor departed; the outdoor amphitheatre grew silent; the fires burned out.

Today, the Maryland Institute of Art, having acquired the building, flourishes inside. In summer, outside on the slopes, crowds gather once again to enjoy concerts. All that remains of railroading at Mount Royal, and the glory days of the Royal Blue to New York is, for those who would have a memory of it and would strain to hear it still, the sound of the conductor's "All aboar-r-r-rd!" shouted out in the late afternoons of old Mount Royal Station, *circa* 1950.

THE LAST
PARKTON LOCAL

AT PRECISELY 6:15 in the cool of the morning of June 29, 1959, the "Parkton Local," the famous commuter train that ran from Parkton near the Pennsylvania line, down through the Jones Falls Valley, eased her way forward, heading ultimately for downtown Baltimore's Calvert Station.

From Cockeysville to downtown the tracks are still there. The 1959 Calvert Station, north of Centre Street, was a makeshift replacement for the famous and ornate original between Centre and Franklin, which had been torn down in 1949 to make room for the present Sunpapers Building.

The "Ruxton Rocket" (one of her nicknames) leaving Parkton, headed for its next stop—Graystone, two minutes away. This would be the final day of the Parkton Local. The Public Service Commission was allowing the service to be ended and the occasion had created a carnival but nostalgic atmosphere.

Russell Mellinger, then a conductor on the run, remembers that "at every stop people came aboard with cameras, and looked for souvenirs."

And so it was at each stop. White Hall (6:24 A.M.), Blue Mount (6:27 A.M.), Monkton (6:30 A.M.). "People were coming aboard I had never seen before," Mellinger says, "and I knew every one of the regular passengers. Matter of fact, every one of the passengers knew one another—they always took the same seat. It was that kind of a train ride."

Now, at 6:32, the train was at Corbett; at 6:35 in Glencoe; 6:37 in Sparks; 6:41 in Phoenix; 6:44 in Ashland; 6:46 in Cockeysville. "Sometimes when a regular passenger was late we'd hold the train and wait for him," says Mellinger. "And when someone left a package on the train at night I'd hold it and give it to him in the morning. I loved that train."

In Cockeysville the crowds got bigger and included mothers with children. Someone who was there remembers that, as the train pulled out for Texas, there was a bouquet of posies on her front light. After Texas, she pulled into Padonia (6:51);

Timonium (6:54); Lutherville (6:57); Riderwood (7:00); Ruxton (7:02); and then into a landscape turning especially lovely as the run went past Lake Roland, the placid water mirroring the green foliage and the blue sky.

Lake at 7:05, Bare Hills at 7:07. In its golden age there were three trains in the morning for the men, a later train for the women shoppers, a theater train at night (it got you downtown for the curtain and home by midnight).

Mt. Washington at 7:09, Woodberry at 7:12, Pennsylvania Station at 7:18. Then the next and last stop at 7:25—Calvert Station and a final, if reluctant, cheer. The celebrating passengers had come to the end of the line.

And so, too, had Baltimore's lurching, lovely "Toonerville Trolley" of a commuter train, the Parkton Local.

THE LAST
LOCUST POINT FERRY

AT PRECISELY 5:00 P.M. New Year's Eve, 1938, Captain Leon Joyss was standing at the rail of the harbor ferry *Howard Jackson*, then tied up at the Foot of Broadway (Fells Point). He barked a command to the seamen to let go the lines, and thus began a historic journey—a four-minute voyage across the Inner Harbor to Haubert Street in South Baltimore. This was the last time the famous Locust Point Ferry, which had seen across-the-harbor service since 1813, would make the run. The old captain, who had gotten the final word only the day before, was skeptical. "Discontinue the Locust Point Ferry?" he snapped. "I'll believe that when I see her tied up. Never happen."

He had reason to be skeptical. From 100 to 400 people a day had been making the crossing for more than a century, beating the long trip and the heavy traffic going the land route around the harbor, using Pratt and Light streets down through Key Highway and Fort Avenue.

But despite the captain's doubts and over the strong objections of the people who lived in East Baltimore (and the Polish people who lived in Locust Point; they insisted they needed the ferry to take their children to the Polish schools in East Baltimore because there were none in Locust Point), the ferry was doomed. Although it had a long history of successfully threading its way through the churning freighters and excursion boats in the harbor and making it to the other side, the ferry was costing the city $25,000 a year. That was more than Mayor Howard W. Jackson believed the taxpayers would go for.

Various reasons were given for the ferry's demise—improved streetcar service, better roads, the automobile as a way of life. Now at about four minutes after five o'clock on that long-ago New Year's Eve, the *Jackson* was nosing her way into her dock, and Captain Joyss was shouting orders to his mates to secure the ferry's lines, making her fast at Haubert Street.

He took time out to say his piece about the whole affair. "It wasn't streetcars or autos or better roads that killed this ferry," he said. "It was the cost of the ride. Right now, it's 3 cents for children, 7 cents for adults, 22 cents for a car. That's just too much money to charge anyone to go to Locust Point."

With that, the captain, knowing the time had come, stepped off the *Jackson* onto the pier and waved goodbye, a sort of Auld Lang Syne, as it were, to the Locust Point Ferry.

Today, half a century after across-the-harbor ferries shut down, they are back—willing and able to taxi you to anyplace along the shoreline of the Inner Harbor you want to go. There's a moral in all of this you should keep in mind when toasting to old times. In the Baltimore Renaissance, don't be too quick to drink to the end of anything. Things have a way of coming back.

THE COLISEUM

L ATE IN THE YEAR 1938, Les Sponsler, then a well-known fight promoter, swung a pick into the frosted ground of a lot on North Monroe Street in an area best identified today as being near Mondawmin Shopping Center. Sponsler was ceremoniously beginning the construction of the Coliseum, which came into being with the high promise that it would bring Baltimore "boxing, wrestling, basketball, tennis, musical events, all under one roof."

In its time, which proved to be short, the Coliseum more than kept that promise. It was, until the mid-'50's, when it closed, the scene of many a wild night of boxing and wrestling. Such improbable specimens wrestled there as Rocco the Acrobatic Italian, the very elegant Lord Carlton, and the Zebra Kid; all before capacity crowds of 3,500 people, according to the newspapers.

It was the center, too, for musical fare. An early photograph shows the marquee featuring "Tonight: Ben Bernie and All the Lads! Tonight!" And in 1951 it was host to "Jazz At the Philharmonic," which brought to Baltimore on one stage Gene Krupa, Ella Fitzgerald (that night she broke up the audience with "How High The Moon"), Duke Ellington, Sarah Vaughan and Nat Cole.

In the 1940's, basketball fans were given bad news: the Coliseum's basketball nights were to be given up for roller skating! Later, though, the Bullets played a season there.

Today the Civic Center holds 14,000; Memorial Stadium, 60,000. Against the background of the gargantuan audiences for sports and rock festivals of the 1970's, the era of the tiny Coliseum seems so long ago. Its closing brought to an end the time when Baltimore's indoor professional sports would be contained in a one-story arena nestled among the row houses and warehouses of North Monroe Street. A sports arena with a capacity audience of 3,500—that's how long ago the Coliseum was!

BRING BARTH BACK
TO BETTERTON

BETTERTON BEACH, that once-and-famous strip of memory and sand across the bay in Kent County, whose glory days faded in the '50's and disappeared altogether by the 1960's, is reaching out for a comeback. The piers that accommodated the excursion boats out of Baltimore, the hotels, the restaurants, the dance halls—all are now in varying stages of decay and disrepair.

But the Mayor and leading citizens and business people in Betterton are staging crowd-drawing events and going after the publicity—all designed, of course, to bring back the people and the good times.

They'd get the job done quicker if they'd just call John Barth of the English department at Johns Hopkins University, leading novelist, member of the National Institute of Arts and Letters, recipient of a Rockefeller Foundation grant in fiction and of the Brandeis University Creative Arts Award—the list goes on.

But in 1948, Barth—*Professor* Barth now, please—was a drummer in Buzz Mallonee's jazz band, playing for the crowds at Betterton Beach.

"The Wilson Line's *Bay Belle* would pull in there a couple of times a day and we'd be on the pier playing," he recalls. "At night, after all the boats had gone, we'd play at the Rigbie Hotel for cocktails from about 4 P.M. to 6:30 or so. Then we'd play every night for a dance from, say, 8 until midnight and beyond."

Buzz Mallonee played the trumpet; the young Barth, the drums. "We were into all that cool jazz," Barth says. "George Shearing stuff like 'The Nearness of You.' Our theme song was 'Embraceable You.'"

Included in the current Betterton promotion program is "Betterton Day," which, according to an account, recently drew a crowd of 2,000. A 14-year-old was crowned "Miss Betterton." The county plans to build a picnic area and a gazebo, a new bath house and a pier. All well and good.

But if these Betterton City Fathers really want the crowds, if they really want to see cottages and condominiums and inns and restaurants, they could do no better than to get Professor Barth to put together, once again after some 35 years, the Buzz Mallonee Orchestra, fix up the old Rigbie and especially its dance floor, turn the lights down low and give Barth the downbeat so that he and his boys can get into "all that George Shearing cool jazz"—in particular, into a chorus of "Embraceable You."

If that doesn't bring the crowds back to Betterton, nothing will.

WHEN HK AT
BELVEDERE WAS NEW

LATE IN THE MORNING of September 12,1948, 93-year-old Max Hochschild (son of the founder) cut the ribbon strung across the doorway of the gleaming new glass-and-brick Hochschild Kohn & Co. "suburban" branch at York Road and Belvedere Avenue. Following a short speech by the president, Martin Kohn, old Max personally ushered in the 2,000 or so people who had come to spend their money.

"It's my new baby," Max kept telling everybody. "It's my new baby." ("New baby" is what he called each of his suburban stores, as they opened, one by one).

The announcement that this very same HK&Co. store was closing was as good a time as any to declare, in the history of Baltimore retailing, the end of the dominance of those famous old family-founded Baltimore "downtown" department stores—Hochschild's, Hutzler's, Stewart's, O'Neill's. They do not tower over the shopper's world as they once did, from the 1930's through the 1950's, before the discounters got big and sophisticated, before the new guys moved in from out of town, before the suburbs with their giant malls and huge parking lots beckoned.

But alas! gone with their dominance is Hochschild's "Toytown Parade" with its billowing balooning Mickey Mouse and Goldilocks and Noah's Ark, and Santa's elves wheeling their little green mailboxes along the curb so that the kids could "mail" their letters to Santa. Gone, too, the Stewart's Christmas windows with their ornate Christmas gardens and angels hovering about; and Hutzler's famous balcony where you planned to meet your family and friends on a Saturday morning. (The store even provided a giant memo book for you to write and receive messages).

Gone, too, is O'Neill's with its unmatched collection of fine linens and its special customer-to-salesperson arrangement: you didn't ask for a salesperson, you asked for *your* saleperson—a Miss Kate, or a Miss Rose or a Miss Lillian.

Gone the liberal exchange policies (it seemed they would take back anything, anytime) and the "charge-and-send" system (you could buy a $1.50 handkerchief, charge it and have it delivered to your door the very next day in the store's own delivery truck).

Max Hochschild's "babies" and all their "cousins" have all grown up now. They are today monstrous emporiums offering huge selections, convenient parking, competitive pricing, superb merchandise.

And having grown up, leaving us the memory of their Toytown Parades and their Christmas windows and easy exchange policies and no-charge overnight delivery of anything, they have left us remembering the best of their childhood.

BROWN'S GROVE

SHORTLY AFTER MIDNIGHT in the early morning hours of July 5, 1938, fire suddenly broke out in the racer-dip ride in an amusement park and bathing beach on Rock Creek, south of Baltimore and slightly west of Fort Smallwood. The blaze, reported as "spectacular," was raging out of control by the time the Riviera Beach Fire Department arrived. A second alarm brought the Orchard Beach Fire Department, but it was too late. Only a pile of smoldering rubble on the shores of Rock Creek remained of the racer-dip, the merry-go-round, the refreshment stands, midway, picnic groves and bathhouse of Brown's Grove.

News of the fire created little stir in Baltimore's largely white community, but in the black community there was much sadness—and nostalgic reminiscences. Brown's Grove was the black community's first, last and only seaside resort.

The late Chuck Richards, perhaps best known locally for his years as an announcer and personality on WMAR-TV, once recalled the era: "We boarded the excursion boat *Starlight* at the Foot of Broadway every Sunday morning and took a lovely 45-minute ride over to Rock Creek and to Brown's Grove. We spent the day picnicking, taking the rides in the amusement park, swimming and boating. Later in the evening, as dusk came on, we took the *Starlight* back—often under the moon. There was a ballroom aboard, and dancing, and always a very good band. Seems to me we did a lot of the Lindy Hopping!"

Both Brown's Grove and the excursion boats (including the *Avalon* and the *Newhill*) were owned by Captain George Brown, who arrived in Baltimore in 1893, a poor unemployed black with, he would say later, "just enough baggage to fill a cigar box." Half a century afterward, he had become the first black member of the Master Mates and Pilots Association, and a prosperous and prominent businessman. Brown died in 1935, three years before the fire burned down his Brown's Grove (and his excursion boats went to the scrap pile), and he never saw how the end came. There can never be another Brown's Grove. A world-within-a-world had gone up in the smoke of the fire that burned on the shores of Rock Creek—45 very long years ago.

"NUMBER PLEASE"

I F YOU WERE living in Baltimore on Tuesday, January 11, 1946 and you picked up your phone to make a call, you discovered (not to your surprise) that it wasn't working. Your neighbor's wasn't, either. Baltimore was suddenly cut off, family from family, business from business, the city from the state, the state from the country. The Baltimore telephone operators had gone on strike. In the days before push-button dialing when most phones were "manual," a strike meant that the ladies who ordinarily greeted you with a cheery "Number please" were not at their switchboards.

These now-famous ladies were always polite, always helpful. You gave them the number you wanted and they "put you through." It was that simple, that pleasant. To this day, those operators (many still alive) tell stories of how lonely widows would call, "just to make sure you're there in case I need you." And how often this call would come through: "Get me to a hospital, I'm in labor."

They worked at exchanges the names of which corresponded roughly to the geography of the city. HOpkins took in the University area; FOrest, Forest Park; VErnon, Mount Vernon; MAdison, Madison Avenue and Bolton Hill; and so forth. Unaffected by the strike were BElmont, BRoadway, CHesapeake, CLifton, FOrest, HAmilton, HOpkins, LAfayette, LIberty, MOhawk, MUlberry, SAratoga, TUxedo and UNiversity. But closed down tight (save for emergencies) were CAlvert, CUrtis, EDmondson, GIlmore, MAdison, PLaza, RIverside, SOuth, VErnon and WOlfe.

Retail businesses that depended on phone-ins collapsed; businesses that had the bad luck to be located in exchange areas that had been struck screamed bloody murder. Housewives, the sick, the disabled, lovers—all pleaded for the strike to be settled. Which, happily, it finally was, two days later.

That was the last telephone operator strike in Baltimore. Today's technology has pretty well eliminated the need for most of those operators. Now in many businesses if

you want to make an outside call it may require as many as 16 digits—and the whole process is automated. It is voiceless; it is bloodless.

And it is all a long way from the days when you picked up your phone and heard a voice, vaguely like your mother's pleading with you to drink your milk, asking, "Number please." Sixteen digits, 26 digits, (126 digits someday, who knows?) will get you your number all right, but it will not get you that voice. You have lost that connection forever.

THE PRE-
SHOPLIFTING DAYS

BALTIMORE REGIONAL PLANNING COUNCIL
Baltimore, Maryland

Dear Sirs:

I see by the paper that you forecast a "revival of neighborhood shopping, thanks to rising transportation costs and a relatively older population."

You should not issue such a forecast lightly. If half of it comes true you are in for trouble. The problem is best illustrated by the story of an incident that happened to Stewart Udall a couple of years ago. Udall, Secretary of Agriculture under Kennedy, was arrested as he was leaving a chain drug store in Virginia. He was charged with shoplifting because he attempted to leave the store without paying for a small pack of cigars (value 95 cents) which he had stuck in his pocket and forgot about. Charges were ultimately dropped, leaving Udall to muse, "Maybe I ought to shop in my neighborhood store, where they know me."

Now if Udall had been shopping in an old Baltimore neighborhood store of the genre the council has in mind, the story would have probably turned out something like this: Udall, in a hurry and thinking long, dark thoughts as all men do while shopping, would have grabbed the cigars and walked right out of the place—unnoticed, unchallenged. Next time in he might have gone up to Doc (or Pop or Mom) and blurted out, "Doc, last time in I stuck a couple of cigars in my pocket and for the life of me I can't think how many or what kind." Doc, scarcely looking up but recognizing the voice, might have said, "Hi, Stew. How's the wife? They take off the cast yet? Cigars? Make it half a buck and call it even."

Today (here is where the trouble comes in) a shopper, accustomed to the rough-and-tumble ways of the giant stores—security guards, TV cameras probing, speed and no nonsense at the checkout counter, no checks, no exchanges—a shopper hardened to all this and suddenly coming across the style of "Old Doc," is going to think the store is a cover-up of some kind and he's going to call the police, who no doubt will raid the place. These raids are going to be repeated at neighborhood drug stores, groceries, bakeries and butcher shops all over town. There aren't going to be enough police to handle the mess; the mayor will have to declare a state of emergency.

You see, you can't take people who are in the habit of shopping at giant chains and send them, willy-nilly, into old Baltimore neighborhood stores. It's too late for that. And don't say I didn't warn you.

Sincerely,
Gilbert Sandler

THE HISTORY OF VAUDEVILLE

EDITOR'S NOTE: Here's a sentimental piece with a little hint of spice for all you Larry, Moe and Curly fans. See if you can spot the reference to the Stooges buried among these recollections.

LADEEEES AND GENTLEMEN! Preee-senting for the first time ever, *Baltimore Glimpses'* very own history of vaudeville in Ball-tee-more! Five memorable acts, five! A star-studded reee-view of famous names and fabulous times! Maestro, if you please, a little travelling music, as we bring you . . .

ACT ONE: We are in Pearce and Schect's Amusa Theatre (414 East Baltimore Street) September 6, 1908 watching Johnnie Jones and his Trained Dogs. The critics would call it, unenthusiastically, "polite" vaudeville, but it is a beginning.

ACT TWO: Vaudeville has caught on, theatres are springing up all over town. There are now, in the World War I years, two-a-day at the Lyceum on North Charles, the Academy of Music at 516 North Howard, the Bijou at 1100 East Baltimore and Blaney's at 315 North Eutaw, where George M. Cohan himself is performing.

ACT THREE: 1920, the Victoria (415 East Baltimore) is featuring Yiddish Theatre, and at Keith's on West Lexington, an act has them in the aisles: "Onaip" (piano spelled backwards) in company with Rajah, a clairvoyant, and a young tenor, Morton Downey. The Maryland (316 West Franklin) is offering the best of the out-of- town circuits including Minsky's (which will fold in Baltimore the day after Roosevelt closes the banks in 1932).

ACT FOUR: In the mid-1930's, vaudeville is packing 'em in at the Hippodrome. One show, in 1939, features Ronald Reagan and Jane Wyman ("A Comedy Team") in Louella Parsons' All-Star Revue. It plays to ho-hum reviews. Felice Iula is running three-a-day at the Stanley; the State on East Monument is raffling sets of dishes between acts. But radio and movies prove too much. Vaudeville, as it does all over America, dies, too, in Baltimore. We are never again to hear the likes of

"Hey Moe, run up the curtain."

"Whaddya think I am, a squirrel?"

You'd think we wouldn't miss that, but we did, and in 1950 there is a revival of vaudeville at the Palace (later the Town). It is short-lived, and stage shows survive alone at the Hipp.

ACT FIVE: At the Hippodrome on the night of May 31, 1951, the curtain comes down on Pee Wee King and the Cowboys as they twang through the last, sad notes of "Tennessee Waltz." The applause rises and falls; the house lights go up, the audience filters out into the Eutaw Street night. Vaudeville is dead in Baltimore.

Well, folks, that's the show. Bring down the curtain, boys, and thanks for the applause. We'll always remember how they loved us in Baltimore!

BAGGY-PANTS
COMEDIANS

DEWEY "PIGMEAT" MARKHAM died not long ago. He was the baggy-pants comedian best remembered for his line "Here Come Da Judge," an inextricable part of a loose and always changing act which he performed on the Gayety Stage dozens of times. The Gayety on The Block was Baltimore's only first-line burlesque house from about the late 1920's through the '60's.

Many people remember the Gayety for its famous—and infamous—strip-teasers: Ann Corio, Lilli St Cyr, Sally Rand, Patti Waggin, Peaches. But afficionados frown on that perception. The baggy-pants comedians were far more interesting, talented, funny.

Dr. Kronkite, to a patient coming out of anesthesia: Do you know who you are?
  Are you Mr. Cain or Mr. Abel?
Patient: I'm Cain.
Dr. K: How do you know?
Patient: Because I know I ain't able.

Mike Sachs was a regular on the baggy-pants circuit and, although few knew it, Mike Sachs was blind. Then there was the famous Dusty Fletcher. Into every one of his skits Dusty would find the time and place to interrupt his monologue and shout upwards to an invisible someone at an invisible window.

Open that door, Richard! Richard, I say open that door!

These comedians would often seize on a line like that and by repeating it often as a non-sequitur in unlikely situations within the skit, draw a laugh from it every time. No one knows the origin of the line,

Slowly, I turn . . .

and although Abbott and Costello are often given credit for that famous routine, all the baggy-pants set used it.

The Gayety was damaged by fire in the early morning of December 21, 1969, and never reopened, thus bringing down the final curtain on genuine burlesque in Baltimore. So all of you who hooked school to go to your first burlesque show at the Gayety; all of you from the country club set who took in the Gayety New Year's Eve Show in your tuxedos; all of you who were Saturday afternoon regulars; bow your heads in memory of Pigmeat Markham and all of the other baggy-pant comedians who played the Gayety and say, in fond recollection of all the times and all the laughs, one last time:

Here come da judge. Here come da judge . . .

THE GREAT
ROYAL THEATER

THIS SONG, ladies and gentlemen—if this old ricky-tick piano holds up and I can see you through all this smoke—hey, you still out there? . . . (light applause)—is a blues song (light piano vamp). A beautiful lady has left my life and yours and, oh how we miss her! I'm talking about the Royal Theater, once on Pennsylvania Avenue.

The Royal opened in 1920 and the biggest names in the world of black entertainment played there. I remember hearing Billie Holliday—she was from Baltimore, you know—singing "I've Found a New Baby," and Cab Calloway, "Minnie the Moocher." Pearl Bailey—big star today, right? In her first performance at the Royal she was only in the chorus line. Sarah Vaughan? Dinah Washington? I heard them all at the Royal (piano vamp).

Well, in the late 1950's and early 1960's the Royal was showing signs of fading. What happened was that the white-only rule was breaking down all over town, television was big and getting bigger and stealing the audience; and of course, the big bands themselves were disappearing from the scene, one by one. The last night—here's to that last night! (quick piano run, "Should Auld Acquaintance Be Forgot . . .")—was January 6, 1965.

No less a musician than the Count himself—that's Count Basie—was playing. As the curtain went up the Count and the boys were already into "Sent For You Yesterday (Here You Come Today)" and the house was going crazy.

Funny thing, though. Nobody knew this was the end, the last time any live show would ever play the Royal stage. The management never announced it, so the audience stood and applauded just as if the great Royal stage shows were going to go on forever. They weren't, though. After the Count finished this one-week gig, the Royal would show only movies. Then, come 1975, the whole building would be torn down to make way for the Upton renewal project.

Well, back to that last night at the Royal. The Count went into "Jumpin' At The Woodside" and I thought the joint was going to go crazy digging that Basie style. Big brass explosions behind a low, murmuring sax solo, a bit of light piano tinkling after the brilliant brass barrage!

The evening moved on. It was time for the last number, and everybody knew that it was going to be "One O'Clock Jump." The band gave it everything it had. I never heard so much noise, from both sides of the footlights. Some of the kids were dancing in the aisles. Well, the curtain came down and the applause died out and everyone left the theater. It was all over. The soul of Baltimore's famous Royal died in those last notes of Count Basie's "One O'Clock Jump."

I told you this was going to be a blues song, but I guess I don't have to sing it for you. You know why I got the blues. . . .

MAIL BY STREETCAR

THE MAIL, to put it charitably, has gotten bad. Horror stories abound; three days to get a letter from Baltimore to Annapolis, five days to New York.

Which calls to mind the story of one Richard Thompson, who in the 1920's depended on same-day delivery! His secret: he knew the speed of Baltimore's "Railway Post Office"—the official name of the U.S. Post Office's "traveling Baltimore streetcar post office," in service until 1929 (Roland Park, St Helena, Highlandtown, Arlington, South Baltimore, Govans).

"Those streetcar post offices really delivered," Norman Yingling recalls. He should know; he was a postal clerk aboard the Towson-Catonsville line. "We had a cancelling machine aboard. We'd pick up mail at the mailboxes along the routes. We'd start out early in the morning, picking up the mail and delivering it to the various neighborhood post offices." With two or three deliveries a day, same-day delivery was assured. Same-day delivery was what Richard Thompson depended on.

That's because young Richard, who lived in Roland Park, was then dating a young lady named Naomi Pritchett, who lived in Govans. It was his habit to mail Naomi a post card in the morning when he went to work. He knew the Railway Post Office would be by promptly, and within hours would have his post card in Naomi's hands. "I would write her in the morning what plans I had for the evening," Mr. Thompson says. "Whether we were going to a movie or out with friends, and what time I would pick her up. When I called on her in the evening, without exception she had gotten my postcard, and she knew my plans for that same evening."

Richard had other plans, too—to marry Miss Pritchett, which he did.

The mail today, unreliable and tardy as it is, not only inconveniences business and politics and publishing, but, the way things are right here in Baltimore, love. For, in the time it takes a steamy letter from a panting lover to get to the object of his love, enough time may have gone by to give her doubt, and to take up with another suitor. So instead of prompt mail bringing people together in marriages, we have slow mail breaking them up.

That's how bad the mail is today.

124

TAPED
CHRISTMAS NOSTALGIA

EDITOR'S NOTE: Here's a creature of the Sandler imagination in the form of a make-believe "recording tape" with the sounds of long-ago Baltimore on it. Like so many of Gil's inventions, this was a device just meant to frame an otherwise disconnected series of recollections. Yet so convincing was it that readers wrote and phoned in to find out where they could get a copy!

WE HAVE A very special gift for our readers this Christmas. It is a tape on which we have managed to record certain sounds peculiar to the Baltimore of 30 or so years ago. As is the case with gifts that you give but would rather have received, we can't wait to share this one with you. So, let's get this tape on the recorder here. Press the "start" button, and here we go:

HeygetchaSunNewsExtraExtra!Readallaboutit! That's the sound of the newsboys at Howard and Lexington. There's more on that same track: *Shopping Bags, five cents;* the tape's still running. Here are other sounds you might recognize:

clangclangclangclang (against the background of traffic noises). That's the streetcar trying to bull its way through Lexington Street. Let's keep the tape rolling.

Waldeemelenlopescawn!...Waldeemelonlopescawn! The cry of the A-rab leading his horse and wagon down a neighborhood street, advertising his watermelons, cantaloupes and Anne Arundel corn.

And what's this sound, people singing? *Oh cut it down, oh cut it down, yes they cut down the old pine tree.* Right! the Rivers Chambers orchestra, popular through the 1950's for proms, moonlights, reunions, singing in chorus the famous theme song that always had everybody singing along.

And speaking of sing-alongs, listen to this: *All right, everybody, let's follow the bouncing ball!* That's the voice of Harvey Hammond, seated in the Century Theater at the console of the mighty Wurlitzer organ, inviting everyone to sing-along to the words projected on the screen.

Those boat whistles you're hearing, *dooo - ooop, do-o-o-o-p!,* those are the excursion boats churning around in the Inner Harbor, on their way from or to Tolchester, Betterton, Norfolk, Richmond, Love Point. And these sounds: *chuff-chuff-chuff-chuff—* do you recognize them? They're the sounds of the trains always on the move through town—the B&O, the Western Maryland, the Northern Central careening up the Jones Falls Valley. And these: *clink-clink-clink*—surely you recall the clinking of the milk bottles as the Western Maryland dairyman delivered the milk to your door at day-break?

Well, I hope you like the tape, and that you play it many times, but just one time shy of the point when the sounds will no longer be audible, where there is just one play left. That way, you will always know that, anytime you want, you can put on this tape and listen to the faint and faraway sound of the 1950's. Now isn't that a lovely present?

Merry Christmas, everybody.

THE VACUUM-
CLEANED PARADE

LATE IN THE AFTERNOON of November 22, 1936 (the day before Thanksgiving) Ben Posen, advertising manager of Hochschild Kohn, was beside himself with anxiety. Here it was, only about 30 hours before Baltimore's first Toytown Parade was to begin, and although just about everything else was in place (bands, Santa's helpers, mail boxes, floats), the huge balloon characters which were advertised as the big draw of the parade, had not arrived.

They were to be delivered by 5 P.M. via trucks out of Binghamton in upstate New York, but when that didn't happen Posen, suspecting trouble, got on the phone. His fears were confirmed. The trucks were snowbound in Binghamton. Worse, even if they could leave early in the morning, it was unlikely they could arrive soon enough to allow time for inflating the balloons before the 9:30 parade start.

Thanksgiving Morning, Nov. 23, 1936, Charles Street near University Parkway: it is a big, wide, noisy parade, filling the street curb-to-curb, and the huge balloon characters are larger and taller than any that parade watchers had ever seen. They were billed as "the largest in the world." The bands are playing "Santa Claus Is Coming To Town" and the drum majorettes are strutting to beat the bands, and Santa's helpers are wheeling their "mailboxes" along the curb so the kids can mail their letters to Santa.

Posen gets assurances that the trucks will leave as soon as the roads are clear. If they leave by 2:00 A.M. they can arrive by 7:00 A.M. But could the Hochschild crew get all those balloons inflated in two hours? There is an outside chance. It is worth a try.

Here comes a towering Cinderella balloon, so big it takes six Hopkins students to pull it along with ropes. Next, a giant Mickey Mouse. Then Goldilocks; then Noah and his ark. Wild cheers break out as each of the balloon spectaculars makes an appearance before another group of watchers, lined six deep along the curb.

Posen is working on an idea—a desperate one. To get the balloons inflated fast he commandeers every vacuum cleaner in the store ("Including," he would recall later, "some right off the sales floor."). Miraculously, the balloons arrive at about 7 the next morning, and a crew of porters, using the commandeered vacuums, works like dervishes to fill them.

By 9:30 the big balloons are moving down Charles Street. Over 200,000 celebrants see the parade this Thanksgiving. For the next 30 years the Hochschild Kohn Toytown Parade would be a major event. But Ben Posen, viewing the passing parade in the sunshine of that long-ago morning, could not know that. He was too busy thinking that this Toytown Parade, which was to become first a tradition and then a rich memory, was only a few vacuum cleaners away from being no tradition at all.

WRONG MCKELDIN HONORED?

NATIVE BALTIMOREANS walking through the new Theodore R. McKeldin Square at Light and Pratt Streets conclude that the area, enhanced with the cascading waterfalls and swirling pools of the Meyerhoff Fountain, is a striking, dramatic architectural showpiece, a spectacular tourist attraction and a delightful urban experience—but that the square is named after the wrong McKeldin.

It takes nothing away from our former and distinguished governor and mayor to remind the City Fathers that, though in his time Theodore R. McKeldin ruled City Hall and the State House, it was his brother, Sergeant William (Bill) McKeldin who ruled this Light and Pratt corner for most of the 1940's and '50's. Unchallenged, too.

Day after day Bill McKeldin stood at Light and Pratt in company with his famous horse, Bob. That noisy and disordered intersection in those days carried one of the highest volumes of traffic in the world, and Bill McKeldin ran it like a general running a battle.

He barked instructions at drivers and pedestrians alike, and by whistling through his teeth, punctuated his orders with ear-shattering blasts. While Bill was working inside the traffic kiosk, Bob, tied up outside, was trained to shift positions with the shift in traffic. So when the signal changed, Bob would move his body to place himself parallel with the traffic flow. He was a living, moving median strip. For managing that trick, Sergeant Bill deserves the Mayor's "Baltimore's Best" award—posthumously.

Walking through the fountain (a gift to the city of Mr. and Mrs. Harvey M. Meyerhoff), among the cathedrals of rushing water, by the glimmering reflecting ponds, and taking in the grandeur of it all, it surely must have occurred to some Baltimoreans that the name of the square ought to be changed. If not to the "Sergeant William McKeldin Square" then at least, to "The Square of the Brothers McKeldin."

LEE DAVIS
"AT" THE GAME

WHEN GALEN FROMME died, a rich repository of the history of old Baltimore radio was lost to us forever. Galen knew all of the legendary Baltimore radio men, and loved to talk about them.

"When I came to Baltimore in 1939," he once told us, "two morning shows dominated. One was WBAL's Bill Herson, who was always writing songs and singing them on the air. He wrote 'I Found My Business in Baltimore' and actually got Jimmy Dorsey to play it at the Hippodrome. He's best remembered for 'When You Buy Better Try Hochschild Kohn.'"

Galen knew Ralph Powers and Phil Christ of WFBR and liked to tell about "Cream Puff," their character who would actually brush his teeth on the air as an inspiration to the kiddies tuned in.

"Al Ross was another WBAL zany. He perfected the technique of stealing taped lines out of previously recorded material—such a line as, 'That's a fat lie,' and then inserting it at an appropriate (or inappropriate) point in his patter or in a commercial."

Galen knew Bill Dyer, Gil Kreigel, Buddy Deane, all of WITH. "Deane was the very first radio man in Baltimore to build a show around popular music." And Homer Todd ("Dialing For Dollars" on WCBM), Charlie Purcell ("Nocturne"—the poetry readings late at night over WCAO); Chuck Richards and "Hot Rod" Hulbert of WITH in the 1940's, the first blacks to broadcast over Baltimore radio.

"But I guess the wildest radio man in Baltimore," Galen recalled for us, "was Lee Davis of WCBM, in the 1930's. Lee did the play-by-play for the International League Orioles. He brought a lot of enthusiasm to his broadcasting of the games, including the 'away' games—*and he wasn't even there to see the action he was describing!* He'd sit in Baltimore, watching code coming in on the teletype from, say, Newark. A message like '2cf' would mean 'double to center field'—that was all Lee needed. He'd go to the mike and go crazy. He'd create a whole scene of action built around that little code message—the screeching line drive, the diving attempt at a catch by

the fielder, the runner sliding into the bag—none of which he saw, and most of which never happened. But it was so realistic that the listening audience didn't know Lee wasn't even at the ballgame."

All of these crazy stories about Baltimore radio men—anybody less than Galen Fromme telling them to you and you wouldn't believe a word of it.

THE ORIOLES' MANAGERS

EDITOR'S NOTE: This next column appeared soon after the 1982 baseball season, when Earl Weaver had retired after 14 years as manager of the Orioles, and before Joe Altobelli got his job.

MR. HANK PETERS, General Manager,
The Baltimore Orioles

Dear Mr. Peters:

I see by the papers that you have a position open, that of Manager of the Baltimore Orioles. I should like to apply for the job, and present my credentials.

You should know that Oriole managers, since the days when I was a very young boy in the bleachers at old Oriole Park on 29th at Barclay, have always looked up towards me in the stands for the crucial "sign"—beginning in 1929 with Fritz Maisel. Once, with the count 3 and 2 in the bottom of the ninth and the Orioles behind 4 to 3 and Mighty Joe Houser at bat, Fritz looked up to me for help and I signalled for Houser to "take." It was a called strike—to end the game and lose it.

I was there, too, when manager Frank McGowan (1933-34) was pitching his ace, Harry Smyth (a 21-game winner the previous year). Smyth was pitching to one of Newark's star sluggers and McGowan looked at me. I signalled "fast ball, low and in." It went out of the park and the Birds lost.

I helped, too, in similar fashion, Oriole managers Joe Judge (he lasted a month) and Guy Sturdy (he lasted until 1936). I helped Sturdy to get the Birds to finish no higher than fifth, despite the heavy work of superstars Woody Abernathy and Pooch Puccinelli.

In 1937 Bucky Crouse came in, and as a player-manager was voted MVP. With my signals, however, he never got the Orioles to come in any better than fourth.

Then Oriole management went big-time and brought in the great Rogers Hornsby and somebody passed the word to old Rog to depend on my signs. It cost him. The Orioles under his management came in no better than sixth.

Then they brought in Tommy Thomas, who managed for 10 years, and some people say if Thomas hadn't picked up the habit of looking to me for signals he would have done a lot better than he did—which wasn't as bad as his predecessors.

It was the same under successive managers. Jack Dunn III in 1949, Nick Cullup in 1950, Don Hefner in 1951, Jimmy Dykes in 1954, Paul Richards from 1955 to '61, Luman Harris for one 1961 month, Billy Hitchcock in 1962 and 1963, Hank Bauer from 1964 to mid-1968, and Earl Weaver. They all counted on me for that critical what-to-do sign. As you can see, I don't seem to have helped them very much, but at least I was there. That ought to count for something.

I look forward to hearing from you.

Sincerely,
Gilbert Sandler

THE VANISHING SHIPS

EDITOR'S NOTE: Here's a column that, for a change, got the illustrator into trouble instead of the author. Reaching for some visual metaphor to express our sadness at the disappearance of so many Chesapeake cruisers, I showed the Smokey Joe *sinking into the water. My mistake, but Gil took the angry phone calls informing him in no uncertain terms that the* Smokey Joe *never sank. It was decommissioned and scrapped. Here, along with a shamefaced apology for my ill-conceived poetic license, is a sorrowful song of farewell to an era of waterborne pleasure.*

BEING A HISTORY *of how the steamboat excursion era came to an end in Baltimore's Inner Harbor: Moonlight, banjos, fine "Eastern Shore" dinners at sea, and dance music.*

1938: The Locust Point Ferry across the harbor to Foot-of-Broadway (now usually called Fells Point) made its last run on New Year's Eve. It provided a four-minute trip 15 times a day, but was costing the city $25,000 a year, and the City Council cut the service. (See page 97 for details)

1939: The *City of Baltimore*, a luxury liner you could take from Baltimore to Le Havre, France (18 days, round trip, $180) was forced out of business by World War II. The Baltimore-to-Fort Smallwood excursions fell victim, too, to World War II. The most popular of the excursion boats to Fort Smallwood, the *Tred Avon*, was scrapped.

1942: The stately white banana-carrying freighters of the United Fruit Company's Great White Fleet were enlisted in the war effort. They would return in 1947, disappear again for good in 1958.

1947: The *Smokey Joe* ferry from Love Point on the Eastern Shore to Pier 8, Light Street, a two-hour-and-twenty-minute run, smoked its last. "Roads, bridges, tunnels," her captain, Norman Taylor, said at the time, "have made all these old Baltimore ferries useless."

1952: The Claiborne-Annapolis and Matapeake-to-Sandy Point ferries running across the Bay ended service, victims of the newly-built Bay Bridge. Average trip across by ferry, 45 minutes. By bridge, 7 minutes.

1962: The Old Bay Line's famous *City of Norfolk* made her final run. Passengers had boarded every evening at 6:00, sat down to dinner, then settled in for an evening of dancing under the stars before retiring to their staterooms. By morning, Old Point Comfort and Norfolk.

1963: All the Tolchester boats—the *Emma Giles*, the *Tolchester*, the *Annapolis*—had by this time gone out of service, bringing to an end not only the day-excursions but the moonlighters, including the *Bay Belle*.

1964: Not a single steamboat excursion boat was to be seen making its way through Inner Harbor traffic. Most of the beaches were closed, the boats scrapped—their dreamy trips down the river and across the bay now only memories, stories parents tell to children.

A newspaper account of the last trip of the *Smokey Joe* records that on that sentimental journey one old-timer was seen at the rail, all by himself, "playing a banjo and singing." The story does not say what this last, lonely remembering figure was playing and singing, but we can guess.

Probably "Til We Meet Again."

RICHMOND MARKET'S
CAT RODEO

O N FRIDAY, July 12, 1929, for reasons not apparent to its mystified and suddenly inconvenienced customers, the Richmond Market, abutting Howard, Read (then Richmond) and Biddle Streets and Linden Avenue, had signs posted on its doors, saying "Closed Today."

What the customers didn't know, and what the merchants didn't want them to know, was that this was the day the merchants were staging, inside the market, their "Cat Rodeo."

You got it right—"Cat Rodeo." That was the name the merchants themselves gave to the event, and an explanation of these strange goings-on follows.

While it was true that the Richmond Market catered to the Uptown Carriage Trade, much as the old Lexington Market did, for too many months previously the market had been fighting a losing battle against mice, and to turn the tide someone thought of bringing in hordes of cats. Only, as it turned out, the cats multiplied so fast they began to out-nuisance the mice.

Then the merchants conceived what they believed to be the ultimate strategy: close the market for a day, round up all the cats and send them to the SPCA. Accordingly, the Richmond Market closed July 12 and the celebrated Cat Rodeo began.

The cats had it won before the contest began. They were nowhere to be found. They hid in corners, under boxes, high in the rafters. Said one observer, "The cats misunderstood the purpose of the round-up."

In the end, it didn't matter. The glory days of the market, in business since 1834, were to be short-lived. By 1950 one more institution had become a victim of the rush to the suburbs, the deterioration of surrounding neighborhoods, the rise of supermarkets. The once-bustling 50-stall market was down to half a dozen stallkeepers in a cavernous, empty hall. In 1959, the wrecking ball did its work. Walk by there today and you'll see a drug store and a part of the Maryland General Hospital—but where did all those cats go?

Occasionally one stray cat will walk by, showing no sign of pride in knowing that for his (or her) progenitors, this was not a market at all. Rather, it was a field of glory where Baltimore's cats soundly defeated Baltimore's Richmond Market merchants, on a day that shall live in infamy—July 12, 1929.

THE LAST
MOVIE PALACE

NOW PLAYING! "The Rise and Fall of the Stanley Theater"
"Tears your heart out"—Donald Kirkley, *The Sun*

REEL ONE: 1927. At 516 North Howard Street, construction is underway on—judging from the giant columns and the towering arched windows—a palace of some kind, rivaling the Taj Mahal. The camera moves us inside. We are walking on gleaming terrazzo floors, inlaid with brass. A winding staircase leads to a balcony thickly carpeted and richly furnished with divans. Maroon tapestries adorn the walls. This *must* be the Taj Mahal. High above is a massive and glittering Tiffany cut-crystal chandelier with intricate gold-leaf decoration. All in all, a study in opulence. With the camera fixed on the chandelier, a fade. The screen goes white.

REEL TWO: We are at the Grand Opening. Gowned and jewelled ladies and tuxedoed gentlemen clink glasses. To the majestic sounds of an organ, guests stroll into a huge theater and take their seats. After speeches and applause, the curtain goes up on Fred Waring and His Pennsylvanians. Next on the screen, "The Stolen Bride." Afterward, an exit march and then this scene, too, fades.

REEL THREE: 1956. We have been watching the construction and opening of the Stanley Theater, an apotheosis in the history of Baltimore movie houses. But now, on our screen, the marquee reads, "Stanton." Now, the featured movie is "Oliver." A wrecking ball is poised to knock down this once-and-famous pleasure dome. It is April 17, and people are reading in their newspapers that the Stanley-Stanton is doomed. The ball connects. In slow motion, in silence, the giant columns and the arched windows come tumbling down. The credit lines roll slowly upward: "The Stanley was designed in 1927 by P.J. Henson . . . built by Stanley Crandell for $2,500,000 . . . on the site of the Academy of Music. The story you have seen is true."

And they are telling you that it is, for the great movie-palace era in Baltimore, "The End."

WRONG-WAY CORRIGAN

DUNDALK AND EAST BALTIMORE had never seen anything like it before. On this sunlit afternoon of August 9, 1938, crowds lined the streets all the way from Logan Field (then the city's airport) into downtown, straining for a view, cheering wildly. And for what? Why, to see Douglas (Wrong-Way) Corrigan, who was in Baltimore, straight from a massive New York ticker-tape parade.

Corrigan was the gee-whiz, 31-year old aviator who flew a tin lizzie of a plane across the Atlantic, landing in Ireland only to claim there that he had been heading for California. Now he was a national hero and Baltimore turned out to give him his due.

In a welcoming editorial *The Sun* offered him the hospitality of the city, and urged him to partake heavily of "Baltimore's famed steamed crabs." The motorcade led to City Hall Plaza where Mayor Howard W. Jackson gave him the keys to the city.

"Welcome to Baltimore, Mr. Corrigan," the Mayor shouted over the din. "I hope you will enjoy your stay, and be sure to eat plenty of Baltimore's steamed crabs."

From City Hall, Corrigan was whisked to the Country Club of Maryland for a V.I.P. reception and dinner—featuring, of course, those famous Baltimore crabs.

Corrigan turned out to be a charmer, telling a couple of good stories—including one in which he said that on his wrong-way trip to Ireland he had looked down through the clouds and had seen far below him an airport by a large body of water. "I thought that was Baltimore," he said, "but I now know that it wasn't."

After the reception it was time for dinner and, of course, crabs. Corrigan took one look at them and turned yellow, all the boyish charm gone. With a slightly wrinkled nose, he said, "I ate one of those once and it made me sick." With that, the chef hurriedly found him some leftover cold chicken—which Corrigan ate with gusto.

Looking back, we shouldn't be surprised at the Corrigan wrong-way saga. A guy who would decline steamed crabs in favor of cold chicken—that's precisely the kind of guy who would take off for California and wind up in Ireland.

THE SANDWICH
MAN

SOME PEOPLE SAY that when the redevelopment around the Lexington Market (the Murdock enterprise, taking in Howard and Lexington, Saratoga, Greene) is completed, "downtown will be back."

That wistful, wishful observation turns on the notion that buildings and glass and fountains and walkways make up a "downtown." It takes nothing away from the planners' dreams to suggest that for Baltimore's downtown to "come back" we are going to need the likes of Jacob Stock on the scene.

Jacob Stock was an advertising "sandwich man" who walked the streets of Baltimore's downtown from the 1930's through the 1950's, enlivening it, and giving it its peculiarly Baltimore tone and mood. There were scores of sandwich men, but Stock, distinguished in his tuxedo, bow-tie, high hat and whiteface clown makeup, was easily the most famous and most familiar.

Those advertising sandwich men were as much a part of downtown Baltimore as were shopping bag vendors, the aroma of roasting chestnuts and Christmas windows. Their advertising sandwich boards were made up of two signs which hung over the man's front and back (making a "sandwich" of him) and were connected by left and right straps which rested on the man's shoulders. The advertisers included such Baltimore institutions as the Oasis Club, Corbi's Restaurant, Read's, Bay Shore Park.

Most of the sandwich men merely walked the streets, letting their signs do the work, but not Jacob Stock. An ex-circus clown, he was a walking clown act. He jabbered away at anyone who would listen, often commenting on the news ("Down with the Commies!"), cracking old vaudeville jokes ("Lady, what did you do with all that money I promised you?"), haranguing taxi drivers and streetcar motormen who jeopardized his street-crossings, and generally breaking into conversations. But he did his job well. One client, the Oasis, seemed to use his services continuously.

Thinking about it all, these new buildings and walkways and fountains going up in the Howard and Lexington area to "bring back downtown" will not bring back downtown. Not for the natives, at any rate. We need the sandwich men walking up and down Baltimore Street, advertising Baltimore's memorable establishments.

All of which prompts *Glimpses* to humbly pass along this advice to the planners— taking into account urban geography, architecture and sociology: Yes, you can bring downtown back to Baltimore, but be advised, without the advertising sandwich men, you can't bring Baltimore back to downtown.

LAKEWOOD POOL

AS CITY LIFE COMES BACK to its former glory, as living downtown and midtown grows more urbane, as the number of people moving back to the city increases and these same people demand more amenities—as all of this happens, it is time to reopen Lakewood.

That is going to take some doing, because that in-town swimming pool at the northeast corner of Charles and 26th Streets has been filled in. Over the bones of its memory now sit several office buildings. There is today not a trace of Lakewood's clear, clean blue-water pool, its sandy beach, locker rooms, snack bar, juke box, diving boards, and beach umbrellas.

In its day, from 1932 to 1944, it was one of the most popular pools in the area. The shallow end was along the fence that to this day runs along the top of the slope high above the railroad tracks at 26th Street. The deep end of the pool was closer to 25th Street.

Not only was Lakewood the favorite of native Baltimoreans but also of the many stars of the entertainment world then appearing at the Hippodrome (among the regulars were Milton Berle and Leo Carillo) and from the literary world, including Scott and Zelda Fitzgerald.

Fred Steiber, who was a Lakewood regular, recalls the days: "There was a miniature golf course at that location in the 1920's which never really did well. But swimming then was a popular sport in Baltimore—the sports pages were full of swimming news. The interest of Baltimoreans in swimming led the Price family to build a swimming pool on that land. Charles and 26th then was a lovely residential neighborhood—quiet, stately, lined with tall beautiful trees. It was idyllic."

As we suggested earlier, reopening Lakewood is not going to be easy. The whole place has been buried for 40 years. But it is an exciting idea to think about, especially as the bulldozers dig deep and start to hit the artifacts that recall the Lakewood era. We can hear it now:

Workman atop power shovel, digging up at Charles and 26th: "Hey Fred, take a look at this!" He points to a shovelful of earth which contains some odd-looking items.

Fred, the helper, makes a hurried examination of the items and remarks, "What in the world is all this stuff? Looks like the top of a woman's bathing suit. And a popsicle stick! A locker key! A beach towel!"

Workman: "Must have been a swimming pool here at one time, huh?"

Fred: "A swimming pool? Here? At Charles and 26th? No way!"

Maybe Fred is right. Maybe there never was a Lakewood swimming pool at Charles and 26th. No blue-water pool, no sandy beach, no snack bar. Maybe it *is* all a dream . . .

LAST JOURNEY
IN "DOLORES"

NOW THAT THE SUBWAYS are running, and running very well at that, old-time Baltimoreans are comparing, inevitably, the new subway system with the old streetcar lines. There are, of course, many similarities, in look and operation and reliability. But if this Metro system is ever to be put in contest as an equal to the old United Railways and Electric Streetcar lines, the subway system is going to have to get hold of its own version of *Dolores.*

Dolores was a funeral streetcar. It came into service in Baltimore just after the Spanish-American War and so the management named it *Dolores*, the Spanish word for "sorrows." Many an old rider, running breathlessly toward the open streetcar doors only to see the car leave without him with doors closed unceremoniously in his face, was heard to mutter, "I'm going to board that damn car if I die trying."

Some people ultimately succeeded and boarded those streetcars dead—as part of a planned, formal funeral. In those days a demand was felt for a more comfortable, more dependable hearse service than the horse-drawn arrangement then in use. Every cemetery, after all, was on a streetcar line. And the funeral streetcar eliminated the occasional danger that a horse might stumble, break its leg, and have to be shot on the spot (It sometimes happened).

The *Dolores* proved to be so popular that it stayed in service until 1927. A unique feature was its construction: two interior compartments, one for the family to sit in, one for the body to lie in. The family could be sequestered behind black curtains, but the casket, thanks to a pane of glass along the forward part of the car, was visible, and the body could be viewed. The *Dolores*, complete with motorman and conductor, rented for $20. If you think that's no bargain, check with your local funeral director.

So for all its gleaming steel and glass and blinking lights and automatic change dispensers and ticket machines, what kind of subway system is this anyway? Truth is, a born-and-bred Baltimorean, accustomed to the amenities of the old streetcar system, wouldn't be caught dead in it.

PURCELL'S "NOCTURNE"

V ALENTINE'S DAY CAME AND WENT THIS YEAR, but the media, it seems to us, despite some imaginative tries, could not properly manage to help us celebrate this festival of love. True, radio stations played "love music"; newspapers gave us recipes for the "foods of love"; TV personalities made small jokes about the world's great lovers. But it didn't work. None of it seemed quite to capture the mood. The problem, at least here in Baltimore, we finally concluded, was that *Nocturne* was off the air.

Organ accompaniment, "I Love You Truly."

> *The sun has drawn its shade across the azure sky,*
> *The night shrouds its veil about the earth,*
> *While the mystic ribbon-like notes of the organ*
> *Merge with the words of the poet.*

That was how Charles Purcell would open the half-hour *Nocturne* show every night exactly at midnight over WCAO, reading his poems of love over the soporific organ playing of Roland Nutrell. We don't know what love poems Charlie read for his Valentine's Day show, but we can guess.

Organ accompaniment, "Silver Threads Among the Gold."

> *How do I love thee? Let me count the ways.*
> *I love thee to the depth and breadth and height*
> *My soul can reach*

The readings originated first from the Century; later, from the Valencia; then from the Parkway on North Avenue. Some years after the show had gone off the air, Mr. Purcell recalled, "Listeners seemed to love it. We went on the air in 1937, and after every show the letters would pour in. During World War II while I was in China and Burma, I used to record the poetry readings on Armed Forces Radio Station,

and send the discs to Roland. He would put them on the air and play the organ accompaniment behind them, just as if I were reading them here in Baltimore."

Plough Broadcasting bought WCAO in 1957 and announced it was establishing a rock-and-roll format, putting an end to 20 years of Purcell and Nutrell and, too, to Browning and to Shakespeare and their songs of love on the airways. The last show was midnight of May 25, 1957. Here are Charles' closing lines:

Organ accompaniment, "Lullaby" by Brahms.

Sleep on, dream on, as the night shall fade away.
There comes a time for us to say, the song is through.
These words of love we at long last end.
Good night. Good night. Sweet repose.

Radio stations today give us "Talk Radio" and "News Radio" and "Adult Radio" and "Country Radio." But maybe one of these days a radio station will give us the kind of radio *Nocturne* gave us—"Love Radio." Pretty syrupy stuff, all right. But maybe that's when Baltimoreans will know again that Valentine's Day has been here, and gone.

THE KIDS' LOCAL
TV HEROES

S O MANY KIDS WERE SWARMING over the slopes of Druid Hill Park near the zoo in that Spring of 1957 that zoo director Arthur Watson asked WJZ-TV to call off its Mister Poplolly contest. But at this point this was easier said than done. Poplolly (one of the screen aliases of Royal Parker) had already done the damage. He had told thousands of kids watching him regularly on TV that he had lost his famous sunglasses out there in the park, and asked the kids to help him find them.

Those were the days when all the stations featured their own local TV kiddie heroes. Stu Kerr was *Bozo;* Richard Dix was *Officer Happy;* Larry Lewman was *Pete the Pirate;* Gerry Wheeler was *Lorenzo;* Keith Heffner was *Mr. Toby.*

But Royal Parker, in his 30 years on Baltimore TV, has been more kiddie-hero personalities than anybody. From the early 1950's until 1957 or so, he was Mr. Poplolly, a sort of cross between a streetcar motorman and Captain Kangaroo. He wore a motorman's uniform with a change-maker around his waist. From there until the mid-1960's he was Popeye, wearing a sailor suit and sailor hat and hosting cartoon guests like Olive Oyl and Bluto. From then until the era died he was P.W. Doodle.

"Doodle was really me as a boy," Parker says. "He was a newsboy on TV as I really was as a boy." Doodle the newsie had his own newsstand where such guests as Mickey Mouse came by. "I never saw myself as educating the kids," Royal says. "I left that job to Sesame Street. I saw my job as *entertaining* the kids."

Apparently, over the years, Royal Parker has been successful at that. These days, 20 years and more later, when the kiddie-hero shows are a fading memory, Royal says that people in their 30's and 40's approach him to say hello, and to introduce him to their own kids. "I can always tell how old these parents are," he says, "by the name they use to introduce me."

So if you were once a TV kiddie-character junkie and, with the years, you've become the type who doesn't want anybody to know how old you are, don't ever introduce your kids to Royal Parker—at least not by the name of Poplolly or Popeye or P.W. Doodle. The world may not know your age, but Royal Parker will.

CHARGE
AND SEND

O N AN AFTERNOON IN THE SUMMER OF 1942, 16-year old Bette Davis (of Baltimore, not Hollywood) was sitting on the steps of her home in the Forest Park section of Baltimore when a friend of the same age happened by. She confided that she awaited a package on the Hochschild Kohn delivery truck. "I bought it yesterday," she said, her anticipation showing. "It'll be out today."

There was nothing unusual in that. Next-day delivery of retail purchases, no matter how small, was part of the "charge-and-send" era of service to customers that seemed to have no limits. Alas, rising costs, increasing distance between store and customer, and the advent of the giant credit card services brought an end to next-day delivery.

The delivery truck Bette was waiting for was part of the many fleets operated by the major retail stores, crisscrossing the town and often making two deliveries in a day to the same house. In those days customers seldom carried their purchases out of the store. Almost everything was put on "charge and send."

Today, if you want to charge, negotiation must take place. You must come to an agreement with the store on a charge plan. A decreasing number of stores still offer their own credit. If you want your purchase delivered—and it still can be—there is often a delivery charge. That delivery is often through a carrier serving many stores. As for when the delivery will be made, that is a matter affected by the day of your order, the season of the year, and where you live. Don't look for it the next day.

But back to that day in 1942 and Bette Davis. The Hochschild delivery truck arrived right on time, and the driver presented Bette with her package. "What is it?" the friend asked. Bette opened the package with obvious pleasure and showed its contents. "Three handkerchiefs! Aren't they lovely?" She had charged a $1.50 item, and the store had delivered it 24 hours later.

Next time you go shopping, try buying a $1.50 item and then saying to the clerk, "Charge and send, please." Make it clear that you expect free delivery—the next day. Be prepared to be placed under arrest.

NO MILK
TODAY

GREEN SPRING DAIRY, one of the last of Baltimore's dairies still delivering door-to-door, has been sold. Spokespeople for the dairy say the new owners will evaluate profits after a year. At the worst, Green Spring would close. If it does, this closing will bring to an end the long and romantic era of door-to-door delivery of milk in Baltimore.

For all practical purposes, and for most Baltimoreans, the era really ended in the 1950's. Those were the last years when, no matter where in the city you lived, milk was delivered to your door seven days a week. In the early years, this was done by horse and wagon, and later, by truck. Toward dawn, if you were a light sleeper, you could hear the clinking of the bottles as the milkman set out your order of milk or cream on your porch or your steps, following the instructions on a note you had left tucked in the neck of an empty bottle—"2 qts white, 1 qt choc, half pint cream."

In the earlier years (before the 1940's) you could hear the milkman's horse clip-clopping, moving along the street the distance of a few houses and then, often without command, stopping. One former milkman, Frank Drager, recalled, "The more you worked with these horses, the more you respected their intelligence."

Drager had a horse and wagon route in East Baltimore, first with Gardiner Dairy, which merged with Western Maryland Dairy which merged with Fairfield to become Fairfield-Western Maryland, all of which came to be known as Sealtest.

In the late 1930's, responding to complaints that the horses and wagons made too much noise too early in the morning, the dairies equipped the horses with rubber horseshoes and the wagons with balloon tires, but even that accommodation failed to stop progress. "Soon," Drager recalled, "route by route, trucks were brought in to replace the horses and wagons. By 1939 all the horse-and-wagons were gone."

A whole generation has grown up without even hearing the clink of the bottles and the clip-clopping of the horses; without ever seeing the note in the bottle set out the night before. If Green Spring closes down and door-to-door delivery comes to an end,

then in memory of the era, there ought to be an empty bottle from one of those old Baltimore dairies placed in, say the Maryland Historical Society. In it ought to be a simple, single note penned officially the night before the last milkman's last door-to-door delivery of milk in Baltimore. It should read, without any ceremonial introduction, "No milk today."

THE BEATLES' VISIT

I T IS SUNDAY AFTERNOON, September 13,1964, around 3:30, and a crowd of teenagers—an estimated 25,000 strong—is milling noisily about the entrance to the Civic Center. "That crowd," Police Inspector Leo T. Kelly, one of those in charge of Crowd Control that day, would recall almost 20 years later, "was always ready to break into panic, but it never did."

The cause of the excitement is the Beatles, that quartet of influential British boy musicians who are in town for a concert to begin at 4:00 PM. It is a time of tension, anticipation and bizarre happenings.

Beatlemaniac Marcia Edelson approaches Kelly and shows him an "official" plaque that, she says, her school has "authorized" her to present to the Beatles in their dressing room. Kelly, who was not born yesterday, suggests she get back into line.

Resourceful Eleanor Livingston, dressed in a maid's uniform, tells Kelly she is the Beatles' maid, and must get into their dressing room at once to help them prepare for their act. Kelly is not amused, and tells her, too, to get back into line.

By 4 o'clock the teenagers are inside screaming and cheering and clapping and weeping. "We knew, though," Kelly says today, "that the Beatles were staying at the Holiday Inn up the street, and that when the crowd came out of the Civic Center they would all break for the Inn. We were waiting for trouble."

Inside the Civic Center the Beatle worshippers are sitting through the warm-up acts. Bill Black does "White Silver Sands." The Exciters sing "Haunted House." The Frog Man belts out "Restless." At long last, the Beatles appear on stage, inspiring an endless ear-piercing *eeeeeeeeeeeeechhhh!* from the crowd, suddenly gone wild. Over the din, they can hardly hear:

She loves me yeah yeah yeah . . .
She loves me yeah yeah yeah . . .

When the show is finally over, it happens as Kelly had predicted. His fears are confirmed. The kids break for the Holiday Inn. The police detail is prepared. The mounties, the dogs, the foot patrolmen do their job well. The crowd, caught up in Beatlemania, never gets out of control—it only stays close to the edge of it.

By 10:00 the Beatlemaniacs disperse and quiet returns to Baltimore Street and Lombard Street, and the city breathes a long, deep sigh of relief—as did Inspector Leo T. Kelly, now retired. Twenty-five thousand teenagers, today in their mid-30's (were you among them?) surely agree: he deserves the peace and quiet.

THE "A & W" DRIVE-IN

IN THE MOOD, ta dum de da da . . .
In the mood, ta dum de da da . . ."
—Glenn Miller instrumental, circa 1942

McDonald's, Roy Rogers, Wendy's, Pizza Hut, Rustler—all offer you a rich fare of hamburgers, roast beef, fried chicken, pizza, salad—served up almost the moment you order. But up to the early 1940's in Baltimore, "fast food" was served up slightly slower but perhaps a bit lovelier at one of the many and busy "drive-ins."

Easily the most popular of them was the Hot Shoppe (sometimes known as the "A & W"—explanation follows) at Park Circle, beside what was then Carlin's Amusement Park. Although there was service inside the Hot Shoppe, the big crowds (mostly the high school and college set) were out on the parking lot, in their cars with the radio blaring away.

In the mood, ta dum de da da . . ."

Moments after you drove in, a uniformed "car hop" would come up to your car and attach a tray to the driver's window. She would take your order—grilled cheese, root beer float, cement-thick milkshakes—return with your food and set it on the tray. You never left your car, an arrangement teen-agers seemed to enjoy.

There was still a third way to be served: at an outside bar (now that explanation we promised) at which you ordered an "A & W"—the brand name for a foamy root beer that was a nickel a mug.

The Hot Shoppe is fused in memory with Carlin's Park itself. An improbable Chinese Pagoda marked the entrance, just to the north. Behind (seemingly overhead), Lindy Planes (named after Charles Lindbergh) careened crazily through the night sky. The Hot Shoppe at this location opened in 1932 and closed in 1951. Or 1952, or even

1956, depending on which source you want to believe. Its founder, however, went onward and upward to create the vast Marriott food and hotel empire.

And while fast food places are indeed faster, drive-ins had their advantage, too. Sitting there in the back seat of a car, sharing a milkshake, a couple could always tune in Glenn Miller on the radio and get

In the mood, ta dum de da da..."

WILLIE GREY
AND THE RAID

O N THE WARM EVENING of June 18, 1954, there was a sudden but familiar commotion on The Block—specifically on the corner of Baltimore and Frederick Streets. It was another raid, this time on the world-famous Oasis Night Club. One by one the strippers, the waiters, the musicians and even the customers (whose names would be listed in *The Sun* the next day, including members of the American Newspaper Editorial Association, in town for a meeting) were herded into the paddy wagons.

As one of the arrested stepped out of the Oasis and into the lights, there was a burst of wild cheering from the Saturday night crowd. The applause was for Willie Grey, for 25 years the MC of the Oasis. Willie, whatever else you say about him—and you could say a lot—had style. He was tall, slender, and always dressed immaculately in well-tailored suits at least 10 years old, and kept his hair combed slick and straight back.

It was part of his MC style to approach someone in the audience—usually someone famous like Jack Dempsey or Bob Hope—get the spotlights on the celebrity, introduce him with great enthusiasm and then ask him to stand up and take a bow. The celebrity would happily oblige and start to rise, only to have Grey shout to him "Siddown ya bum, who d'ya think you are? Siddown!"

On the night of the raid the cheering for Willie didn't stop until he had disappeared into the wagon, accompanied by no less a personage than the head of the Vice Squad, Lieutenant Byrne.

This was not the first time the Oasis had been raided for "indecent exposure" during its shows. The club boasted the "World's Worst Show," but those who honestly believed it was, and said so out loud, had to deal with two husky bouncers named Machine-Gun Butch Gardina and Little (6-foot-7) Jack Horner, who would escort them up the stairs and out onto Baltimore Street. There they would forever lament their unfavorable opinions about the Oasis' "Beef Trust"—16 lovely ladies, some of them, as Willie would put it, too late for Social Security.

But back to the night of June 18, 1954. As Willie Grey got into the paddy wagon he was joined, as we have mentioned, by Lieutenant Byrne. Observers recall that as the two of them were crouching into their seats on the bench within, Willie, with a wry smile on his lips, said something to Byrne. History does not tell us what those immortal words were, but we can guess.

Probably "Siddown ya bum. Who d'ya think you are? Siddown!"

SKATEMOBILES

INSTRUCTIONS on How to Build A "Skatemobile," published by *Baltimore Glimpses* in response to popular demand.

If you don't know what a skatemobile is, you didn't grow up in a Baltimore City neighborhood and it is too late in the game to explain it all to you now. But if you did (1930's? 1940's? 1950's? 1960's?), pay attention.

1. You will need a wooden crate (an "engine") about 2-1/2 feet long and about 18 inches wide and about as deep; one roller skate; a 5-foot length of 2x4 (the "chassis"); hammer and nails. (We will talk about "accessories" later.) You can find a box—an orange crate is best—on the back lot of any grocery; the 2x4 from anyplace construction happens to be going on. Steal the skate from your sister.

2. Pull the skate apart. You will now have the front section with two wheels, the back section with two wheels. To the rear end of the 2x4 nail the front section. The front end of the 2x4 gets the rear section. Make certain that the skate sections are securely in place, and will not slip to either side. Slippage could cost you a victory in a skatemobile race later on.

3. Now take the "engine" (the orange crate) and nail it to the front end of the 2x4 (the "chassis") and see to it that the front end of the crate is more or less flush with the front edge of the 2x4. You now have a body of which Fisher would be proud!

4. Now for the accessories (what the auto dealer calls "options"). For headlights, two tin cans, each open at one end, and containing a candle, fixed to either side of the engine. For steering, a right and left handle nailed to the top of the engine. Attach foxtails to the end of each handle for special effect.

And there she sits, a gleaming beauty, 15 pounds of coiled energy! She only appears to be fragile. Believe me, for all of Detroit's moonshine about engineering, it has yet

to match the styling or the nerve-shattering, out-of-control speed of a skatemobile. But now that you've built it, what are you going to do with it?

5. At dusk, after dinner, wheel it off your porch or out of your yard and go careening down the street (candles lit, foxtails flying) by the house of the prettiest 13-year-old on the block. If the sight of this magnificent machine doesn't make her swoon, you have not followed instructions. Go build a model airplane.

KING OF THE
"MONKEY-GRINDERS"

THIS IS A STORY about children and love, and music and springtime, and a Baltimore dimly recalled now through the gossamer veil of years. It begins, like all such stories, long ago and far away. In the French Quarter of New Orleans in—oh, say 1939—we can't be sure, it is early March and Luciano Ibolto (or Louisiani Ibolito, depending on which account of his life and times you read) is standing on a corner cranking out "Whispering" on a hand organ. With his other, non-cranking hand, he holds a leash, at the end of which is his monkey, Julia.

Julia is busy collecting coins from children and stashing them in her pocket, but Luciano is looking up at the sky. Some ancient calendar deep within him tells him it is spring back home in Baltimore now, and that he should be going there.

And so we next see Luciano and Julia on a sun-drenched spring afternoon on the corner of Howard and Lexington, or on the grassy slopes before the flowering shrubs in Mount Vernon Place. Luciano is again grinding out "Whispering" on his hand organ and Julia is again busy with the children gathered around her. She clashes little cymbals, smokes a pipe, picks up her hat with her tail, dons spectacles, combs her hair, salutes men in uniform, preens before a mirror. All the while, she is collecting coins and putting them carefully into the deep pockets of her red jacket.

Luciano Ibolto, who lived in Baltimore at 812 Duker Court, was one of dozens of such "monkey-grinders" (as they called themselves) who every year, after the dark and ice of February and March, suddenly appeared into the sunshine of Baltimore's glorious April. It was how you knew it was spring.

Another way was the bursting into bloom of the red tulips and yellow forsythia in Preston Gardens, but that sign was apt to prove deceptive by expected "unexpected" frosts. It was known that Luciano had discounted these frosts and thus was more reliable.

The last time Luciano Ibolto and Julia were seen downtown was in 1945. Today in Baltimore, in different kinds of springtimes, there are no more monkeys in red jackets performing on street corners for children. Both the children and the organ grinder with his song of love are gone. No wonder, these later years, it's been so hard to know when spring has come.

FOOTBALLERS FOUGHT– STUDENTS, TOO

POLICE LAST NIGHT, the news report in *The Sun* of November 25, 1928, read, "evolved an elaborate plan to keep parading students of Baltimore City College and Baltimore Polytechnic Institute apart on the eve of their annual football game. Forty-two were arrested, five hospitalized, and one police sergeant was left nursing a black eye. One co-ed was left weeping."

November's City-Poly game was the oldest (ultimately, 90 uninterrupted years) and most intense rivalry in the history of Baltimore high school sports. Over the years, the matchup generated enthusiasm and vandalism without ready parallel this side of the Super Bowl. Even now, only some of the stories can be told.

It became a tradition on the Monday following the game to cut school and go downtown to the Hippodrome or the Gayety. Between features, groups of students from both schools would rise up and serenade their respective alma maters, accepting a pelting with eggs for standing up and being counted for dear old City (or Poly).

It was routine for City students to visit Poly's North Avenue campus and paint on the sidewalk, in 6-foot letters, "Beat Poly," and for Poly students to respond in kind.

Once, things got so bad that the student governments of both schools had every member of the respective student bodies sign a pledge to abstain from pre-game and post-game demonstrations. The pledges turned out to be as meaningless as pledges of abstinence during Prohibition. The shenanigans continued unabated.

They even picked up in fury through the 1940's and into the 1950's, when the rivalry was finally swallowed up in the larger pageant of city and county high school sports.

Still, when City and Poly classes get together for reunions, they invariably recall what happened the night before or the Monday after the City-Poly games in their time, enlarging their tales in the telling. Old grads toast the paint and the stink bombs and the eggs. They weep for and with that "weeping co-ed," whoever she was and wherever, in the afterglow of the passing years, she has gone.

NICKEL TOWN?

TRAVEL WRITERS, CELEBRITIES AND ORDINARY PEOPLE, singing the praises of the new, glittering Baltimore are forever comparing it to the old Baltimore. "Nickel Town," they call it snidely, or "Washington's Brooklyn." People riding through on the train see the back porches of East Baltimore flash by.

But people who were born and raised in Baltimore from the 1920's through the 1950's have a different recollection of the town. They remember the good life of summer nights in the amusement parks—Carlin's and Gwynn Oak. They recall streetcar rides to Bay Shore; excursion boats to Tolchester, Chesapeake Beach and Betterton, and the moonlight cruises down the river.

They went to the most extravagant of movie houses—Stanley, Century, Valencia, Hippodrome, Royal. The best of Broadway came to the Club Charles and the Chanticleer. Baltimoreans of those days went dancing at the Dixie Ballroom, saw legitimate theater at Ford's, laughed at burlesque in the Gayety.

They travelled to New York on the luxurious overnight Pullman sleeper; to Norfolk and Richmond on the old Bay Line steamers; to the Eastern Shore and Ocean City on the *Smokey Joe* ferry via Love Point. Streetcars took them everywhere comfortably and dependably—in weather that would shut the new Baltimore down cold.

You could get your hat blocked, your knives sharpened, your shirt collars turned. There were concerts in the park, department store Christmas windows, Thanksgiving Day parades, boxing matches at the 104th Regiment Armory, wrestling at the Coliseum, ice hockey at Iceland and the Sports Center, and baseball at Oriole Park.

What's so "Nickel Town" about all of that? Does this kind of city sound like "Washington's Brooklyn?" Think of all those poor ignorant travelers sitting on the train, streaking through town at 60 miles an hour, staring at the back porches of old East Baltimore, and think about what they missed.

Can we help it if they were too dumb to get off the train?

THE GREAT BALTIMORE
TRIVIA GAME

Once a year, in early May, *Glimpses* takes a break from its usual format. Its faithful readers are challenged on that occasion to display their knowledge of Charm City's past by submitting their answers to a 10-question Trivia Quiz.

We look upon this reproduction of some of those quizzes as an appropriate way to end the book, because if you've been paying attention, students, this quiz will be a breeze for you, and you'll qualify as a genuine Glimpsomaniac.

If you want to know how you rate, you can keep score. Since some questions are harder than others, we have given each question a "Degree of Difficulty" rating, so that the really tough questions give you more credit than the easy ones.

After you've totaled up your score, compare it with the ratings listed below, and you'll know just how crazy you are about Charm City. Remember, now—no cheating!

TO RATE YOURSELF, COMPARE YOUR SCORE WITH THIS LIST:

400 POINTS: The Mencken Award! You're Baltimore's Best.

350 POINTS: The Sandler Award! You're older than you look.

300 POINTS: The Yaniger Award. You're a certified native.

200 POINTS: No award. This is barely passing. Spend a few hours at the Enoch Pratt Free Library, or re-read this book more carefully.

100 POINTS: Really! Why did you bother?

LESS THAN 100 POINTS: Go back to New York and don't ever let me hear from you again.

THE QUIZ:

1. *(5 points)*   Where is the Mansion House?

2. *(10 points)*   Who won the match race between Seabiscuit and War Admiral?

3. *(20 points)*   What was the route of the Baltimore double-decker bus?

4. *(20 points)*   Name the judge and the police official who scourged the bookies of the 1940's and 50's.

5. *(10 points)*   Name the buildings that housed Baltimore's three rooftop night clubs.

6. *(10 points)*   Name the organist who conducted the sing-alongs at the Century Theater.

7. *(10 points)*   Who was the voice of the International League Orioles in the 1930's, broadcasting over WCBM?

8. *(10 points)*   Give the last names of the former strippers at the Gayety whose first names were Hinda, Margie, and Patti.

9. *(10 points)*   Where were the terminals for the Locust Point Ferry?

10. *(3 pts ea)*   Name the streetcar lines that terminated at:
    (A) Howard Park
    (B) Back River
    (C) Manhattan Loop
    (D) Irvington
    (E) Towson

11. *(40 points)*   Al Capone, the famous Chicago gangster, lived in Baltimore while he was being treated at a hospital. In what section of town did he live during this time?

12. *(20 points)*   What Baltimore cemetery operated its own streetcar line from entrance gate to gravesite?

13. *(5 points)*   Which of Baltimore's railroad stations had rocking chairs in the waiting room?

14. *(10 points)* Where was Baltimore's "Arcade"? Through which building did it run and from which street to which street? Describe.

15. *(10 points)* Who was Mayor of Baltimore before McKeldin (his first term) and whose administration ended with the election of 1943?

16. *(5 points)* Which department store at Howard and Lexington Streets featured in its Christmas window the famous laughing Santa Claus?

17. *(10 points)* Who was Avon (Azey) Foreman?

18. *(20 points)* Over which Baltimore radio station was the *Quiz of Two Cities* broadcast?

19. *(5 pts ea)* Connect the cocktail lounge with the hotel:
    I. Hunt Room   a. Southern Hotel
    II. Algerian Room   b. Hotel Mt. Royal
    III. Chesapeake Room   c. Emerson Hotel
    IV. Spanish Villa   d. Hotel Stafford

20. *(10 pts ea)* Which number streetcar would you take to get to:
    a. Carlin's Park?
    b. Bay Shore Park?
    c. Gwynn Oak Park?

21. *(20 points)* The B&O Royal Blue train out of Camden Station to New York did not actually go to New York. To what city did it take you?

22. *(10 points)* What was the Knothole Gang?

23. *(10 points)* Governor McKeldin's brother was a sergeant in the Baltimore police force. His name? (and, for an extra 5 points, his horse's name?)

24. *(40 points)* Name the street where Cab Calloway lived in Baltimore.

25. *(5 points)* Where was Hopper McGaw?

26. *(10 points)* Who was the Bentztown Bard, and what was his real name?

27. *(10 points)* Who (or what) was *Dolores?*
28. *(30 points)* The 34-story building on the southwest corner of Baltimore and Light, now the Maryland National Bank Building, opened originally as the _____ Building.
29. *(20 points)* Who was "The Man With Red-and-Green Eyes"?
30. *(10 points)* To what point on the Eastern Shore did the Love Point Ferry run?

THE ANSWERS

1. The Mansion House is in Druid Hill Park.
2. Seabiscuit the winner, War Admiral paying nothing to place.
3. The double-decker ran North-South on Charles Street.
4. Judge Sherbow and Captain Emerson.
5. The Stanley Theater, The Southern Hotel, and the Keith's Theater.
6. Harvey Hammond. (No relation to the Hammond Organ people)
7. Lee Davis. NOT Bill Dyer.
8. Hinda Wassau, Margie Hart, Patti Waggin.
9. The ferry ran from Fells Point to Haubert Street.
10. A. 32
    B. 26
    C. 5
    D. 8
    E. 8
11. Mount Washington
12. Loudon Park
13. Mount Royal Station
14. The Tower Building. The Arcade ran from Baltimore Street to Fayette Street (or vice versa, if you prefer.)
15. Howard Jackson.
16. Hochschild Kohn
17. Baltimore's flagpole sitting champion.
18. WFBR
19. Id; IIb; IIIc; IVa
20. a. 5; b. 26; c. 32

21. Jersey City, N. J.
22. Give yourself the full score for either of the correct answers to this question, and a double score if you knew both the answers. The Knothole Gang was a program instituted in 1931 by the Baltimore Orioles, wherein any kid could gain free admission to the park for a number of selected games. Later, after the Orioles had joined the American League, a new Knothole Gang was formed, but for a different purpose, It was a television baseball show for kids, presided over by Bobo Newsome, a much-traveled pitcher with "child-appeal."
23. Sergeant Bill McKeldin and his horse, Bob.
24. Madison Avenue
25. At the southwest corner of Charles & Mulberry streets.
26. Folger McKinsey, the Bentztown Bard, conducted a column for the *Morning Sun* which was always introduced with this verse:

    > *It was only a glad "good morning"*
    > *As he walked along the way*
    > *But it spread the Morning Glory*
    > *Over the livelong day.*

27. *Dolores* was a streetcar used strictly for funerals.
28. Baltimore Trust Company
29. Henry Barnes, Baltimore's first Traffic Commissioner.
30. Love Point, of course.